Praise for *Talking*

"At last someone is taking on Dr. Phil with good sense and great humor. Life isn't a sixty-minute show where people just come in for the laying on of hands. Life is about working it all out with family, community, and love. Good for Mr. Bedrick to decide to pull off the gloves and have an emotional slugfest with an over-the-high-school bully. *Talking Back to Dr. Phil* is a must read. But not at dinnertime...you'll be laughing too hard to eat."
—NIKKI GIOVANNI, Poet, Distinguished Professor at Virginia Tech University, seven-time NAACP Image Award recipient

"David Bedrick understands that real change or transformation requires challenging accepted dogma and then approaching problems with compassion and curiosity. He is a great advocate for stopping the madness of body hatred and dieting."
—JANE R. HIRSCHMANN and CAROL H. MUNTER, Authors of *Overcoming Overeating* and *When Women Stop Hating Their Bodies*

Praise for *Revisioning Activism...*

"Teacher, counselor, and attorney David Bedrick is the ideal guide to lead us through new doors of activism. His diverse background allows him to freely pull together issues such as shame and conflict in relationships, and the social sufferings of racism and sexism, all the time urging us to see and create the world anew. His new book, *Revisioning Activism*, helps us critically think and feel through a world in need of individual and social change, bringing depth, brilliant insights, and new strategies to heal ourselves and the world around us."
—ARNOLD MINDELL, Ph.D., Author of *The Deep Democracy of Open Forums* and *Sitting in the Fire*

"Bedrick is a 21st century healer who acknowledges and honors the often epic struggle shared by individuals and groups who triumph over trauma. His theoretical framework is only one significant aspect of the skill and wisdom with which he addresses some of the most central issues of contemporary times. He deploys a psychology of transition and transformation for its potential ability to help individuals, organizations, and even nations navigate the shifting terrain of our changing times."
—ABERJHANI, Poet, historian, and co-author of *Encyclopedia of the Harlem Renaissance* and author of *The River of Winged Dreams*

"As one who has journeyed eastward, marched with MLK, studied and taught psychology and theology, I deeply appreciate *Revisioning Activism's* contribution in service of sanity, justice, love, and mercy. Bedrick's clarity and heartfulness deepen and enrich. He is a true treasure in our midst."
—HERBERT D. LONG, Th.D., Dipl. PW, Former dean and Francis Greenwood Peabody lecturer, Harvard University Divinity School, and adjunct faculty member, Marylhurst University

"We are living in precarious times that often leave us holding our breath and wondering when the other shoe will drop. Covering a broad range of topics and social issues while delivering a fresh perspective, Bedrick has produced a powerful, thought-provoking work. His essays are filled with valuable insights that will enlighten, inspire, and challenge you on multiple levels. It's a gift of awareness, courage, and hope that you will savor and turn to time and again."
—MARY CANTY MERRILL, Ph.D., Author and editor of *Why Black Lives Matter (Too)*, President & COO, Merrill Consulting Associates, LLC

"I'm so glad David Bedrick wrote this book. In the vein of James Hillman's *We've Had a Hundred Years of Psychotherapy and the World's Getting Worse*, Bedrick's insightful, challenging, and brilliant collection of essays in *Revisioning Activism* is an even more powerful clarion call to see individual suffering through a social lens. With unflinching courage, Bedrick looks at tough issues—sexism, racism, anti-Semitism, and homophobia—and doesn't just challenge us to see how society and psyche are intertwined, but provides solutions. Throughout the book, he provides stories, examples, and insights into what can be done. This is something that activism all too often misses. In this way, Bedrick truly revisions activism. He doesn't only call for a better world; he gives us a bridge to get there, offering us powerful new ways of thinking and doing to make the world he's envisioning."
—JULIE DIAMOND, Ph.D., Organizational consultant, coach, and author of *Power: A User's Guide*

"*Revisioning Activism* is a rare read that reveals the essential connections between individual psychology, social history, and societal marginalization. These essays provide a needed education as to how marginalized groups are targets for projection and systemic annihilation, and compromise everyone's mental health. Since his first book, *Talking Back to Dr. Phil*, Bedrick continues to speak to the societal obsession with "normalization" and how this misses the uniqueness of who we are, dampens creativity, and limits our collective growth. Bedrick's passion is palpable, his personal stories compelling, as he gives voice to an activist-oriented psychology that brings together personal work with world work."
—DAWN MENKEN, Ph.D., Psychotherapist and author of *Speak Out!* and *Raising Parents, Raising Kids*

"*Revisioning Activism* takes us into uncharted territories and breaks through the classical boundaries of politics, health, spirituality, and social divides, with an incisive underlying and unifying vision of these disturbances making us more whole. His love for language and his courage to call out his truth makes this book a great and stimulating read."
—MAX SCHUPBACH, Ph.D., President of Maxfxx
and the Deep Democracy Institute

"David Bedrick has a refreshing and often underappreciated understanding of what it takes to achieve greater success with weight loss and healthier living. Most people know that to be healthier, they need to improve their diet and increase their exercise; but sometimes that is an impossible task. Bedrick understands this and realizes it is more about the psychology of weight loss and what drives the individual person to eat what they eat, and how to uncover those deeper meanings. His years of experience and passion for the topic will certainly yield incredible results."
—ADAM PUTSCHOEGL, M.D., Fellow, Pediatric Cardiology, Mayo Clinic

"*Revisioning Activism* offers a radical take on common personal and societal problems that invites us to illuminate our private thoughts and feelings as well as the social context in which these problems arise. Covering topics as diverse as racism, body image, and forgiveness, this book will challenge your belief systems, open your eyes to new perspectives, and bring depth and heart to any process of change."
—GAIL BRENNER, Ph.D., Author of *The End of Self-Help: Discovering Peace and Happiness Right at the Heart of Your Messy, Scary, Brilliant Life*

"Bedrick's compassion and understanding of the human condition brings me back to his teachings time and time again. Whether discussing gender, race, body image, or sexual inequality, he speaks to the heart of the matter and impresses upon us the strength of overcoming our own inner 'Goliath.' Rather than running from our fear, frailties, and so-called flaws, Bedrick empowers us to find the wisdom in our wounds and use it to our advantage. David Bedrick is a powerful, humble, and astute teacher. I highly recommend this book!"
—CRYSTAL ANDRUS MORISSETTE, Founder of the S.W.A.T. Institute and author of *The Emotional Edge*

"From collective social justice to the psychological shadow carried in each of us, Bedrick makes a convincing case for a new sort of activism. Urging critical thinking, less moral judgment toward others, and much more inclusivity, he offers provocative ideas, well-told stories, intelligent and heartfelt observations about the human condition, along with plenty of suggestions for how to get started. A wake-up call for therapists, counselors, and psychologists, as well as a primer for anyone who cares about making a real difference—beginning first with themselves. This is an important book."
—MELANIE HARTH, Ph.D., Psychotherapist and "Living From Happiness" public radio host

ALSO BY
DAVID BEDRICK

Talking Back to Dr. Phil:
Alternatives to Mainstream Psychology

REVISIONING ACTIVISM

*Bringing Depth, Dialogue, and Diversity
to Individual and Social Change*

Essays By

David Bedrick, J.D.

BELLY
SONG
press
Santa Fe, New Mexico

Published by: Belly Song Press
518 Old Santa Fe Trail, Suite 1 #626, Santa Fe, NM 87505
www.bellysongpress.com

Managing Editor: Lisa Blair
Editor: Kristin Barendsen
Book design and production: David Moratto

Revisioning Activism: Bringing Depth, Dialogue, and Diversity to Individual and Social Change is factually accurate, except that names and minor aspects of some essays have been altered to preserve coherence while protecting privacy.

Printed in the United States of America on recycled paper

Publisher's Cataloging-in-Publication Data

Bedrick, David, author.
    Revisioning activism : bringing depth, dialogue, and diversity to individual and social change / David Bedrick.
    Santa Fe, NM : Belly Song Press, [2017] | Includes bibliographical references and index.
        ISBN: 978-0-9852667-8-3 (paperback) | 978-0-9852667-9-0 (PDF) | 978-0-9966603-4-1 (Kindle/Mobipocket) | 978-0-9966603-5-8 (Epub) | LCCN: 2016944067
        LCSH: Social sciences. | Social change--Psychological aspects. | Social justice. | Social advocacy--Psychological aspects. | Change (Psychology) | Social psychology. | Popular culture. | Body image--Psychological aspects. | Weight loss--Psychological aspects. | Racism--Psychological aspects. | Current events--Psychological aspects. | BISAC: SOCIAL SCIENCE / Popular Culture. | PSYCHOLOGY / Social Psychology.

LCC: HM1033 .B43 2017 | DDC: 302--dc23

1 3 5 7 9 10 8 6 4 2

*"We are who we are because somebody loved us.
To be is to be loved."*
—Cornel West & BMWMB, *Never Forget: A Journey of Revelations*

Contents

SECTION II

Hunger, Self-Hatred, Failure, and Sexism: The Real Weight-Loss Story

SECTION III

What's Going On? Reflections on Current Events

SECTION IV

Beyond a Popular Psychology: Remembering the Shadow

Acknowledgments

I must begin by acknowledging the true companionship Lisa Blair, my partner, marital and otherwise, brings to me each and every day. Her tender heart and tireless creative spirit gift me with an ever-present spirit of deep belief in myself, including my writing. She has read, edited, and formatted, countless times, each of the essays in this book, and dialogued with me about the ideas until they arrived in the state you, the reader, find here. I grew up in a rather brutal world; Lisa teaches me, every day, that life can be different. It's been thirteen years—I am slowly learning.

My body and soul were brought into a humble consciousness, about who I was as a white man and as a Jew, by four black elders. First, Maya Angelou's voice, grown in the years of silence following her childhood rape, was perhaps the first true voice I ever heard. *So that is what a human being is capable of,* I thought. *I too want to follow the path of my own humanity.* Second, the dark intelligence of Etheridge Knight's poetic presence nourished me in his Boston apartment, affirming in my Semitic features and the rhythm in my rendering of his poems, the color in my body and soul. Etheridge taught me that desperation was part of the human condition; he taught me not to be ashamed of being a "cracked vessel." Third, James Baldwin's eyes seared through America's façade while still

loving her. I committed to keeping track of America's blind innocence since reading the letter he wrote to his nephew over 25 years
ago. Baldwin's father teased young James about his bulging eyes,
leading James to lie with coins on his eyes, hoping they would re-
cede. Thank G-d those eyes accepted their calling and not his father's jealousy. Finally, scholar, activist, and writer June Jordan
showed me to the door of the essay. Jordan's social brilliance and
lyrical power keeps reminding me of the soaring possibility of voice
and education through writing.

A patience that I am still learning to appreciate was awakened
in me by the tremendous spiritual and radical activist vision of
Meridel Le Sueur. In 1986 (she was 86 years of age), after hearing
her poetry reading, I stepped toward the stage wanting to meet her.
She was in the midst of a conversation some feet away when she saw
me. She walked over to me, put her arms around me. Unexpected
sobs emerged. "Are you still writing?" I asked her, knowing that she
published one of the first feminist novels, *The Girl*, in 1930. "Yes,
more than ever." "Why more than ever?" Her truth entered my being:
"I finally know what I want to say."

In 1992, Arnold Mindell heard my childhood story—really heard
it. He took me on as his student and has minded my path and well-
being for the last 24 years. To think I have been eldered by his love
and psycho-spiritual genius is a privilege that I am still shy to admit
having in my life. Arny's process-oriented psychology flows through
everything I have written here.

Growing up with a father too often violent, and a mother ill-
equipped to respond, was not the sort of gift I desired. But it is the
one I got. That childhood, with years of alchemical cooking, awakened a desire for love and justice borne of that condition. My parents also left me with a kind of inheritance, a deep hope that I would
have what they did not. Though their visions were more material
than the one that called to me, I know that those visions were informed by the same love that holds every marvelous creation. They

are both long gone from this earth, but we still talk often. Their spirits accompany me on my path, making it possible for me to have penned my second book.

In the last two years, my insight about diversity, humanity, and the human heart has been shepherded by Reverend India Elaine Garnett, a woman of grace-full intelligence, worthy of high respect. Thank you, dear friend, for accompanying me with your ever-loving presence.

Perhaps my greatest understanding and compassion has flowered under the tutelage, and urgent needs, of my students and clients, who bring to me their greatest hopes and gifts as well as the truth of their suffering. They have trained my heart and mind, especially those whose difficulties were less amenable to change—they deepened the ground of my being in their life and death.

And how can I acknowledge all that cares for me, without acknowledging the music and poetry that escorts me into states of being beyond words? John Coltrane, T. S. Eliot, Antonio Machado, Rainer Maria Rilke, Joy Harjo, William Butler Yeats, Chicago Mass Choir, Marvin Gaye, The Allman Brothers, Meg Christian and Cris Williamson, Patti LaBelle, and innumerable others. Music and poetry reliably bring the rain when my soul is parched from working too hard and becoming too rigid in my endeavors and ambitions.

Finally, so much is due to a worldwide community of learners who follow a course of individual depth and social awareness. My days are often softened, held, stretched, or engaged in the fires of conflict in ways that remind me of my need for others—that my wholeness is not only an inner project (despite my powerful introversion).

Introduction

In a sense, I was born an activist. Some of my earliest memories are of moments when I spoke truth to power. But my activism has developed along an unusual trajectory. It's an activism born more of the mind and heart than of marching feet. An activism expressed not by a megaphone or signs but through teaching, writing, and facilitating dialogue. An activism that embraces our individual and collective shadows rather than oppressing them or fighting against them. A revisioned activism.

During the past three years, I have developed this revisioned activism through teaching, working with individuals and groups, community building on social media, and writing essays and blog posts for *Psychology Today, The Huffington Post,* and other publications. I see all these venues as opportunities for effecting change. Many of the essays in this book were previously published in these venues.

These essays critique the failure of popular psychology to learn from marginalized people and from the parts of our psyches that are marginalized. They also critique American society's relative denial of the suffering caused by racism, homophobia, anti-Semitism, sexism, and other -isms. They are meant to provoke dialogue.

This Introduction is longer than most, but for a reason. It serves as a kind of manifesto for the book, laying out the central thesis that connects the essays.

I begin with a few personal stories that show how I got here: how and why I became an activist, and which important teachers and artists influenced my thinking along the way. I recount how I came to write my first book, *Talking Back to Dr. Phil,* which responds to many of the current problems I see in mainstream psychology.

I then define *revisioned activism* and explore its three domains: inner activism, social activism, and psychology. I examine how the field of psychology supports the status quo of both individuals and society. I conclude with a brief tour of the four thematic sections that form the structure of this book.

A Nascent Justice Consciousness

I was born in 1955, one year after the U.S. Supreme Court ruled, in *Brown v. Board of Education,* that separate is not equal, and that racial segregation of public schools is unconstitutional. This momentous decision implies a psychological understanding that marginalization itself, even in the absence of any other overt form of discrimination, is injurious in the way it perpetuates the view that some folks are "less than" others.

By the time I was six years old, I was already trying to protect my mother from my father's harsh words and temper. Of course, I didn't have the power to do that, but it upset me more to see her victimized than to absorb his blows myself. I knew that something was wrong with him, and even as a young child I took to debating with him about why he behaved so brutishly.

I now understand those early fights as the awakening of my sense of justice. I saw a grown man misuse his power against a woman and children (my brother and me). One of our chief flashpoints was money, which he constantly worried about. I began to think about the impact of money—its deeper meaning, the way we let it signify the worth of other humans, and the background societal values that drove my father deeper into fiscal anxiety.

When I was 12, my mother, with my fervent support, left my father for six months. Perhaps encouraging her escape was an inappropriate role for a 12-year-old boy. But the heart of that boy trying to save his mother is still with me, albeit with more conscious and wise strategies.

A few years prior, I began Hebrew school, where my fascination with justice and activism was activated. When the rabbi said that Jews are "chosen" people, I winced and hurt inside—I could only think of my best friend Jimmy, whom I dearly loved. Jimmy was Italian and Catholic—what about him? Was I better than him? Was he not chosen? As with my father, I began debating the rabbi. Perhaps he could have explained it to me in a way that bore witness to Jimmy's worthiness and beauty, that honored my love for him, but he did not. I was asked to leave the school.

My parents enrolled me in a new Hebrew school. I was on high alert, ready to challenge the values I found offensive. When I did, I was asked to leave that school as well. Now, as a teacher of some 20 years, I have a particular affection for students who challenge me.

In 1969, when I was 14, my parents urged me to apply to Stuyvesant High School, a public school that accepts intellectually gifted students from all over New York City based on test scores. But it wasn't Stuyvesant's quality of education that made my parents so adamant—it was the fact that *Brown v. Board of Education* had resulted in bussing students across town as part of a solution to ending the segregation of schools. My parents fretted that I might get bussed to a "black school" or that many black students would now be bussed to my local high school. I fought bitterly with my parents over this issue, in part because their racist attitudes were so clear to me. It injured me to hear their words. I took it personally, the same way I took my father's angry words and fists.

Important Teachers in My Life

As my race consciousness flowered, I found that black writers, poets, and musicians spoke to me in a way that other people didn't. My first black teacher was Maya Angelou, whom I first heard speak in Minnesota some 30 years ago (see my tribute essay, "In Honor of Maya Angelou: This Caged Bird Sang and Sang"). She greeted the audience in six languages, all of which she spoke fluently. Even before she said anything meaningful, I could hardly hold back my tears; they were silent sobs in a release I didn't then understand. This grand educator neither hid her light nor the resonant truth of her voice. "That's what a real person sounds like," I heard myself say in a whisper.

I spent the next 30 years studying the dynamics of racism, and I found many black teachers and elders who deepened the education of my heart and mind in ways I will be forever grateful for, in ways that have opened me to the suffering of the human condition and the incredible possibility of being human.

Though I grew up in a Jewish home, we never spoke about anti-Semitism, the Holocaust, or Jewish history. Many Jewish families shy away from the pain of their past, preferring to focus on the more privileged condition of living in the United States today. I understand this orientation; I accepted it with only moderate debate until I studied clinical psychology at the Process Work Institute under the tutelage of Dr. Arnold Mindell. Mindell linked significant aspects of my history, including my father's struggles with violence and money, to my Jewish background.

Later, I told the Swiss psychologist Dr. Max Schupbach the story of my father's physical violence. With tears in his eyes, Schupbach responded, "I can't only condemn your father. I am Swiss, and I grew up in a country that denied its complicity with the Nazis' purpose. Perhaps if I [as a member of Swiss society] didn't participate, your father would have been different." It was one of the deepest moments of healing I've ever experienced—and one I would never have expected. Schupbach had linked social reality to personal reality and psychology.

Mindell, the founder of process-oriented psychology, nourished my soul with a psychology that was not based on normalization or preserving the status quo. With his Jungian orientation and connection to the wisdom of shamanism, physics, and Taoism, Mindell taught me that difficult emotional experiences, like depression, cannot be totally separated from the sufferer's social context. A person with depression may, for example, be dropping down as an unconscious strategy for escaping an oppressive social context. From Mindell I also learned that psychospiritual interventions, such as recommending forgiveness, are not always appropriate for people who are working through an abuse story. Forgiveness can suppress the feelings that naturally arise in response to being harmed.

Mindell also spoke of "deep democracy" (a philosophy of inclusion that not only attended to each person, but also to the diversity of states and feelings people experience) and psychology's role in furthering democracy in both inner and outer realms. He spoke of addicts, homeless people, and "mentally ill" people as shadows of the city who hold a unique consciousness for the rest of us. He showed me how physically ill people have unseen gifts, and he taught me how to unfold and reveal those gifts as a kind of healing.

Mindell has worked with diverse groups of people on social and global conflicts, from sexism and racism in America to the relationship between "First World" and "Third World" countries. He has brought, into the same room, Palestinians and Israeli soldiers, Jews and Germans, LGBTQ folks and fundamentalist Christians, and other opposing groups. When I began my apprenticeship with Mindell, I was 36 years old and my passion for learning soared. This is what I had always wanted to learn. Since then, Mindell's teachings have informed my vision of psychology as an activist tool.

I am now on the faculty of the Process Work Institute in Portland, Oregon, and Warsaw, Poland, teaching process-oriented psychology and working with clients worldwide.

My father died when I was 40. Writing his eulogy, I reflected on how his intellectual gifts never flowered because he didn't have the chance to go to college or otherwise further his education. Because I had always been interested in justice, democracy, and the Constitution, I vowed not to inhibit my own learning, and I applied to law school. I practiced law for 10 years, mostly doing pro bono work through a family law clinic for those who could not afford legal representation. While learning the law helped to develop my understanding, practicing law was unsatisfying to me, as I saw how ineffective the legal system is in influencing the hearts and minds of those who contribute to individual and social problems.

Women have also been my teachers. Many women over the years have opened my eyes to the conditions that women suffer under and through. Some are writers and artists, and many others are students and clients who shared their stories with me. At 46, I began an eight-year teaching tenure at the University of Phoenix. I taught courses in ethics, sociology, psychology, and law, but the class I loved most was critical thinking. I asked students to write a paper about a personal challenge, applying the teachings from class to more deeply understanding that challenge. I was surprised when several of the women students wrote about their struggles with weight loss. As a result, I began a research project where I interviewed 20 women, over time, to further understand the nature of their struggle with weight loss. It became clear to me that internalized sexism was a critical factor in their dislike of their bodies and their desire to change them. Even more importantly, I found that as women become more empowered, they often go off their diet, seeming to sabotage their efforts but in fact rejecting a program that was built, in part, on body shame and hatred. The essays in this book on diet and body image are informed by these women and the stories they shared with me.

My First Book

My practice and study of psychology deepened in my fifties, when I became more and more distressed by the direction popular psychology was taking. That distress found a target when I began watching the *Dr. Phil* show, in which psychologist Dr. Phil McGraw practices what I call a "How's-that-working-for-you psychology." Too often he moralized and put people down rather than look for deeper psychological understanding. Further, he demonstrated virtually no understanding of sexism and racism when he worked with women and black folks. In response, I wrote my first book, *Talking Back to Dr. Phil: Alternatives to Mainstream Psychology*. Affirming the need for activism targeting popular psychology, Nikki Giovanni, seven-time winner of the NAACP Image Award, wrote, "At last someone is taking on Dr. Phil." Carol Munter and Jane Hirschmann, authors of the groundbreaking *Overcoming Overeating*, wrote that I was a "great advocate for stopping the madness of body hatred and dieting."

REVISIONING ACTIVISM

Activism has been defined as vigorous actions to achieve political and social goals. Activists confront institutions that treat people, animals, or the environment in biased or injurious ways. Iconic activist groups include Greenpeace and, more recently, Black Lives Matter, who aim to change both policy and public awareness. People march, protest, speak out, sit in, strike, lobby, petition, block whaling boats and bulldozers, rally against nuclear power plants, and highlight racial injustice. These and other actions are absolutely critical in promoting change in our world.

Perhaps these actions share a common heart—one that seeks to create a more just planet, where voices with smaller megaphones and audiences can be amplified and heard. In this way, activism is core to a thriving democracy. Nevertheless, there are many opportunities for activism—venues, moments, strategies—that are also available to us, but that we tend to miss.

With this book, I aim to re-vision and expand traditional activism. I explore new insights and strategies that expand the tools available to us, and I hope to honor and empower those who are thus far unrecognized for their heroic work. This could include:

- A woman who is looking in the mirror, no longer blind to her beauty
- A Jewish man who is beginning to understand his family violence in the context of anti-Semitism
- A middle-class white man who is starting to recognize that addiction is not just a problem on the streets or in other families—but in himself, his own family, and the culture at large
- A black teenage girl who is beginning to see through the veil of denial and recognize racism's stark cruelty
- A media that highlights the use of performance-enhancing drugs by one particular athlete as well as how we live in a performance-oriented culture that promotes coffee, Ritalin, and other stimulates from womb to tomb
- The millions of other people who are starting a dialogue with their family, friends, and social groups, hoping to build deeper relationships and a more loving community

It is time for professionals in the field of psychology—especially popular psychology—to take a critical look at our profession and its complicity in social distress. Mainstream psychology contributes to individual and social problems by normalizing and accommodating society's status quo, by denying the value of our shadow sides, by encouraging us to project those shadows onto "others," and by ignoring the effect of social injustice on the psyches of people of color and other marginalized groups.

Below I outline three domains into which I hope to expand

the reach of activism, either by bringing awareness to insufficiently recognized areas of activism, or by calling for new strategies and venues of activism.

I. Inner Activism:
Activism Within the Individual Alone

Traditional definitions of activism do not include the moments when we, as individuals, sit privately with our own thoughts and beliefs. However, such moments can be ripe and powerful. Consider the following:

- A woman stands before her full-length mirror. Society's objectification informs her vision, bringing body shame and body hatred to her experience of herself. Research indicates that she may literally see an image larger than her actual body.[1] She decides, yet again, to go on a diet.
- A man faces a powerful depression each morning when his alarm wakes him. He puts on his clothes, a relatively happy face, and a functional-looking outfit for work, stuffing down his depression. He avoids examining his feelings, even though he feels a silent resentment and despair about his job and the way he is treated at his workplace.
- A woman goes to a party, has a glass of wine, and experiences a rare freedom to speak her mind. The next morning she berates herself, "Why did I talk so much? I'm so embarrassed."
- A Jewish college student suffers from family pressure to make a success of himself. He feels anxious every day. His mantra becomes, "I have to get over my anxiety."
- A black woman is corrected by her white manager at work. She gets irritated with her boss, but shortly after is even more upset with herself for feeling irritated. "I'm so paranoid," she thinks. "My boss was just doing her job."

Many of us silently agonize as we wrestle with our demons, without consciously connecting our individual suffering with the social factors that feed it. This lack of context isolates us, so that we don't see the millions of others who are living the same experience for many of the same reasons.

For example, the woman criticizing her body sees herself through a sexist lens. She is unaware that her critical eye belongs not only to her, but to the patriarchy—and that she has internalized a bias that injures women everywhere. The depressed man, who is also oppressed by a culture fixated on harmful gender stereotypes, sees himself as weak—just as many men do when they don't feel "up," productive, and providing. The woman who speaks her mind at the party is used to keeping her controversial opinions to herself because society says women should be pleasant and pleasing at all times.

The Jewish college student grew up among family members who are scarred by a history of anti-Semitism and who now overcompensate for their former status as second-class citizens. The black woman is not paranoid—she knows in her soul that racial animosity and bias inform the tone and particulars of the criticism she faces daily.

These are not only personal moments—they are social and political moments. They are moments when great forces work against us, manifesting in depression, self-hatred, shame, and self-diagnosis. They are moments of potential activism.

When we remain blind to these forces, a moment of activism is lost. When we awaken to them, we not only empower and love *ourselves*, we become more empowered and loving in our world. We become more enlightened and effective agents of political and social change.

When we think of activism, we don't think of these moments. I have worked with many women who are aware of social factors like the glass ceiling, the gender pay gap, the epidemic of domestic violence, and even the media's role in creating body image problems. But these same women still stand in front of the mirror, deciding to wear vertical stripes or certain colors to feel more attractive and confident. Instead of holding society responsible, these women pathologize *themselves*, thinking they have a self-confidence or self-esteem issue, perhaps seeking personal growth in a form divorced from social awareness.

All of these people suffer alone, believing their pain is personal, believing that something is wrong with them. All live a moment that is ripe with the possibility of an activism rarely acknowledged—an inner activism where they can confront the social forces that live and breathe inside them. If they become conscious of their social context and how it manifests in that moment, they will be empowered to heal their suffering. And in turn, they may inform and challenge their friends, family, and community members to be more aware, to bear witness with the eyes and heart of justice.

I remember completing my first year of night classes in law school. Our class had started as 20 men and 20 women. Now, six women and one man were dropping out. I made a point of asking each person why they were leaving. All six women understood themselves as lacking in intellect, readiness, or an ability to apply themselves. They had each tried and convicted themselves of their individual lack. None mentioned the patriarchal style of the old professors, whose sarcasm masqueraded as a Socratic teaching method. None mentioned the fact that only one woman regularly spoke up in class, and that she was derided by all as being harsh and cold. I eventually went to the dean of the law school, a woman who taught a course in power and privilege, and expressed my findings and concern. She didn't even know that six women and one man had left; she had not considered the impact of sexism.

What if these women had realized that their lack of confidence was not separate from a sexist teaching atmosphere? It was an activist moment when I spoke to the school dean. But each of these women had a moment for potential activism when they considered dropping out. They believed their struggles were theirs alone, but if they had seen themselves in their social context, they could have understood that their difficulties came from a bias outside, not from a weakness inside. This could have spurred a moment of inner activism that would not only bring more self-love on the inside, but would also empower them to be change agents on the outside.

We, as individuals, need to remember to ask, "How is my suffering like that of others; what is the social context?" This question reveals that our difficulties are a function not only of our individual psychology, but also a function of sexism, racism, classism, anti-Semitism, or other social injustices. It's a strategy that de-isolates us as individuals and makes working on ourselves an empowering social action.

II. Social Activism:
Actions That Change Culture and Consciousness

Traditional activism often focuses on confronting mainstream biases and assumptions, especially when the injury caused by these biases can be corrected by legislation, consumer boycotts, altered employment practices, shifting the gender or color of faces in the media, or simply awakening the public to suffering hidden from our view. This is crucial work that must be expanded, so that bias, injustice, and injury can be made ever more visible where it is not. Following are four locations and expressions of bias and injustice that are worthy of examination in order to further develop the field of activism.

Media Scapegoating: Creating Shadows[2]
Media commentators have a feeding frenzy when celebrities' vulnerabilities and psychological struggles are revealed. They hold up Lance Armstrong as a symbol of dishonesty, Philip Seymour Hoff-

man as a symbol of addiction, and Robin Williams as a symbol of depression—as if these celebrities are facing challenges that are theirs alone, not difficulties we all confront on some level.

While the media discussion does bring attention to psychological issues, it also supports the attitude that such problems are "out there"—that we, and a majority of people in society, are not liars, addicts, or suffering from depression. In essence, we scapegoat these few, which allows us to project our own difficulties onto them. This kind of media presentation furthers the marginalization of our individual vices, creating a shadow in communities of "others" whom we regard as sick, immoral, or criminal—people who are not us.

To that point, our productivity-obsessed culture advocates performance-enhancing drugs in schools (Ritalin) and at work (caffeine), and a growing percentage of children are cheating on tests to keep up.[3] It's not just Lance Armstrong; we are praised and rewarded for doing anything we can to get ahead, compete, succeed. Focusing exclusively on Lance Armstrong turns us away from the mirror that will reveal that we are him.

Mindell brought a brilliant light to this notion in his book *City Shadows: Psychological Interventions in Psychiatry.* He noted that people who display extreme behaviors are actually fighting battles that the rest of us disown—they embody our collective shadow. If we insist that "they" are pathological and "we" are sane, we are complicit in fostering these dysfunctions. More insidious is that we develop a mindset of superiority that frees us to subject "them" to the pain of marginalization and injustice. If those individuals are to heal, we must all face our own shadows.

A revisioned activism shows us that we are woven together by a common humanity, that the problems are both out there *and* in here—in our own hearts, minds, relationships, and communities. A revisioned activism shines a light on our collective shadows, insisting that we own our vices. The goal of this action is to create social change at a deep level—so we see that we are, in fact, the other.

Individualizing Pathology: Neglecting Societal Responsibility

Much that is written about addiction, anxiety, depression, and stress implies that these are individual problems—not ills that are profoundly embedded in and promulgated by our culture's biases. In the process of scapegoating some individuals as the ones who carry "illness," we become blind to the background systemic variables that foster such illness. These variables include cultural biases, forms of neglect, and marginalization patterns—societal ills that our activists' eyes must clearly discern.

Consider the problem of depression, an illness that leaves many feeling like failures in a market-driven culture that values high energy, productivity, and progress. Our societal bias puts an undue burden and judgment on people who feel depressed. The pressure created by this bias can keep people from turning inward when deeper feelings call them away from the outer world and their current activities. If they ignore the impulse to turn inward, they may be more likely to develop health problems, incite conflict in their relationships, or turn to substances as an alternative way to leave their narrowly defined track. Resisting the happy-face culture is a worthy cause of a revisioned activist.

Our culture also devalues altered and liminal states. We proudly affirm logical minds and rational behaviors and diminish the value of deep emotion, unseen connections, and all kinds of seemingly subjective experiences. The result is that many use substances, from alcohol to food to heroin, to satisfy their need to connect with liminal states, albeit in less conscious and acceptable ways. Viewing ecstasy, dreaming, and even rage as states that are critical to creating a thriving human experience: This is another worthy cause of a revisioned activist.

Or consider the number of people today who suffer from the lasting effects of profound trauma caused, for example, by sexual abuse, domestic violence, or military combat. These individuals are typically seen as just that—individuals—and cultural denial about trauma keeps some from making obvious connections between battlefield violence and veteran homelessness and suicide. Instead, many see an individual who is sick or even deserving of contempt.

Further, many are also blind to the traumatic impact of centuries of violence done to Native and black bodies and psyches. Mainstream Americans invoke a kind of convenient amnesia when we think, "That was 400 years ago, 100 years ago, 50 years ago. Why can't they get over it?" This collective denial means that we fail to understand expressions of these wounds today in the forms of angry protest, poverty, family violence, and substance abuse.

Our marginalization of injury and trauma feeds into the suffering of abuse survivors, battered women, war veterans, and more. A revisioned activism must work to enlighten the culture at large to the causes and impacts of trauma. A revisioned activism uses moments of individual suffering as windows on the cultural biases and ignorance that have played a role in creating these sufferings.

Highlighting Laws and Rules of Behavior: Neglecting the Hearts and Minds Behind Social Injustice

Traditional activism sets out to change political policy and social behavior, but it falls short of changing our collective hearts and minds. The limits of this focus couldn't be better illustrated than by the Civil Rights Movement's magnificent efforts to end Jim Crow segregation. Perhaps one of our society's finest hours was the conclusion reached by the Supreme Court in *Brown v. Board of Education*. With *Brown*, the Court overturned its own 1896 decision, *Plessy v. Ferguson*, which declared that segregated institutions (from schools and utilities to health care and housing) were "separate but equal." The *Plessy* ruling had made hard law out of America's segregated life for black Americans. *Brown* overturned that ruling, though it took decades to enact the Court's decision.

Today, many would argue that our schools, cities, and certainly our churches are just as segregated as ever. Clearly, we are still moved by factors other than love and justice; clearly, traditional activism did its job, but there is still much work to be done.

A revisioned activism must focus on enlightening both perpetrators and victims. It must illuminate subtle forms of bias, found in language and micro-aggressions, not only so we can eliminate these assaults and insults, but also because these micro-injustices reveal the beliefs that underlie our great social ills.

Further, a revisioned activism must focus a narrow lens on perpetrators' denial and minimization of the injuries they cause. For example, America's law enforcement system routinely perpetrates heinous racial injustices, a topic that traditional activism is taking on. However, the law enforcement system's denial and minimization of its role in these injustices causes further injury, often retraumatizing victims and allowing the injustice to remain alive, unseen, in American hearts and minds. Revisioned activism refuses to tolerate this status quo.

Validating the suffering of targets of injustice is another important role for revisioned activism. Too many people suffer from low self-esteem, dysfunctional relationships, financial instability, and health problems, all of which are caused—at least in part—by injustices they suffer under. When people don't see that causal connection, they blame themselves for their difficulties. This serves to empower the assault and disempower their resistance and their ability to be change agents in their inner and outer realms. But the very act of seeing and validating injuries is a healing balm on the psyches of injured individuals and communities.

In summary, activism must do more than work to change policy and behavior. It must also work to change the way people think and feel. If it doesn't, our capacity to make sustainable changes in ourselves and our world will too readily reach its limits. We will set the bar too low.

Bringing Dialogue and Diversity to Activism

Traditional activism gathers people together who have a common interest, vision, or purpose. Activist groups therefore tend to have a homogenous social identity and political viewpoint, excluding those with different perspectives. For example, the moderators of Facebook pages devoted to social justice will often intimidate, verbally assault, and even block participants who express opposing viewpoints. The same attitude holds for groups that meet in person. The advantage of including only like-minded people is that the voices within the group are supported, validated, and protected. There is a kind of solidarity and safety among kindred spirits. People are empowered in this way.

However, there is a serious limit to these activist groups. While they may foster the spirit of diversity in the world, within themselves they often lack diversity, not just of viewpoint but also of skin color and socioeconomic background. Dr. King noted that Sundays were perhaps the most segregated day of the week; it appears equally true that activist groups are among the most segregated groups in our society.

A revisioned activism supplements traditional activism by gathering together people who have strongly divergent viewpoints. Groups formed of great diversity have several key advantages. Some people learn to speak out even more strongly when they are met with strong opposition. Others who have less confidence in their own voice benefit from watching others model how to engage and speak up. Both these types of people become more firm in their beliefs and more empowered social change agents—a good thing!

Equally valuable is that some members learn to listen to people who oppose their position, even listen with a kind of love. This is the practice of non-violence. Learning to listen to those in opposition can not only be a great power and strategy for changing our own opinions and those of others, but it can also foster critical thinking and help people to deepen, broaden, and clarify their views.

Finally, the act of sitting in the fire of opposition educates some folks in how to mediate conflict. They become facilitators of democracy and communication in a world where polarization is rampant. In my view, building community across great differences is perhaps the greatest activist calling of our time. It is not about getting people to change their minds, but about learning how to build sustainable relationships, how to create a more perfect union.

The first time I clearly saw the power of bringing together people with great differences was in the late nineties. About 150 people had gathered from the LGBTQ community and the local evangelical Christian community. These groups were in fierce opposition, and the conflict was hot. Evangelicals quoted Bible verse, speaking about the evils of homosexuality. LGBTQ folks spoke about the evils of discrimination. It seemed no one was going to change their minds about the legislation they were there to discuss.

However, as the conversation continued, people from both sides spoke with more vulnerability. Some spoke about their fears for their children because of abuse they had suffered as children or adults. Others told stories of being the target of anti-gay discrimination.

As the meeting was coming to a close, consensus and change still seemed hopeless. But then I noticed that people from opposing sides were walking out alongside each other and talking about their children. There was a palpable warmth and regard for each other. Indeed, no one had changed their minds—which is the hope of traditional activism. But many had come to see their opponents as humans who were not totally unlike them. Projections lessened; regard and respect were nurtured. Their children, their very humanity, were the common ground they found. No minds were changed, but a taste of community could be felt.

During the past two decades, Drs. Arnold and Amy Mindell, founders of Process Work (process-oriented psychology) and World-work, and Drs. Max and Ellen Schupbach, founders of the Deep Democracy Institute, have been hosting dialogues between people from opposing sides in hotspots around the globe. They have brought together Israelis and Palestinians, white and black South Africans, Aboriginal and white Australians, Russians and Poles, and more. In these gatherings, there is no one person or group who teaches about the marginalized perspective. Neither is there an intention to get people to compromise. Instead, people are encouraged to express their strongest views and feelings. Facilitators hold these often hot conflicts by keenly observing changes in tone, body language, and other dynamics.

When dialogue itself is an activist goal, the advantages are threefold. First, dialogue makes it possible for anyone with family, friends, a social media network, or any other type of community to be an activist. Second, the learning is immediate and powerful when people can bear witness to the impact their statements and attitudes have on others. They can see the anger on others' faces, the hopelessness in their bowed postures, the confusion in their silence, the pain in their tears. Finally, it shows those with dominant personalities what it feels like to be afraid to speak up, to be shot down in public, to not be heard. These experiences can build empathy around what it is like to have more or less power than another—a quality that is essential for all issues of marginalization and injustice. To quote Drs. Max and Ellen Schupbach, it can create "unity in diversity."[4]

III. Psychology:
An Activist Tool and a Venue for Injustice

The field of psychology is having a growing impact on the culture at large. The *Psychology Today* website has millions of readers, and most articles (especially the popular ones) focus on personal growth absent societal forces. Books about personal growth typically emphasize individual healing, divorcing themselves from the cultural context of our suffering and neglecting to address how the process of becoming a political change agent can be an important part of personal growth.

In my view, the field of psychology could be a robust agent of cultural change. But popular psychology tends to support the culture's status quo instead of taking on the role of activist in the world. Popular psychology is biased toward maintaining an inner status quo, helping individuals re-establish the supposed wellness and comfort they enjoyed before their current difficulties.

However, I believe that psychological difficulties are a call for change, not restoration. In fact, our inner and outer worlds often mirror each other—the factors that suppress us inside may reflect the factors that marginalize us in the outer world. For example, given that our culture values conventional and material success, if our passions direct us toward non-mainstream professions (such as art and writing), we may have to deal with our inner resistance even before we take on the outer resistance.

This problem was powerfully illuminated by the late psychologist James Hillman in his book *We've Had a Hundred Years of Psychotherapy—And the World's Getting Worse.* Hillman said to *LA Weekly*, "We still locate the psyche inside the skin. You go *inside* to locate the psyche, you examine *your* feelings and *your* dreams, they belong to you. Or it's interrrelations, interpsyche, between your psyche and mine.... We're working on our relationships constantly, and our feelings and reflections, but look what's left out of tha.... What's left out is a deteriorating world."[5]

To address the impact of a deteriorating world, psychologists, counselors, and all those who value psychological growth must devote more of our resources—teaching, writing, working with clients, and conducting research—toward helping people contextualize their struggles. We must also more strongly support non-normative emotional states, such as depression and rage, without labeling and pathologizing them too readily. And we must be sure to broaden our reach beyond speaking to a white, middle-class, heterosexual audience. Following are three areas in which psychology can manifest its activist calling.

Normalization: Psychology's Support of the Culture's Status Quo

Western psychology has always been biased towards supporting the culture's status quo. Freud frightened mainstream medicine (that is, white male doctors) by declaring that many psychological symptoms result from repressed memories of childhood sexual abuse. Later, under pressure from his peers, Freud abandoned this theory, promoting another that was more acceptable to the mainstream culture—that children had sexual fantasies of abuse, not repressed memories of actual abuse.[6] Psychology thus served the culture's status quo, closeting the epidemic of child sexual abuse and serving an anti-child and sexist agenda.

Perhaps there is no better example of psychology's hurtful bias than when the profession supported mainstream projections of deviancy onto a group of people—homosexuals. While there was no scientific basis for regarding homosexuality as a mental disorder, homosexuals were nonetheless diagnosed. What was considered a sin or an "unnatural act" by mainstream culture, psychology turned into a mental illness. (In 1973 the American Psychiatric Association, "confronted with overwhelming empirical evidence and changing cultural views of homosexuality," removed homosexuality from its diagnostic manual.[7])

Diagnosing, labeling, and treating homosexuals was not just an error of judgment—it served a homophobic agenda, however unconsciously (though one would think that psychologists would be aware of the unconscious).

The brilliant psychologist Salvador Minuchin understood this dynamic within the context of the family system. He noted that those individuals who deviate from their family's norms, and who most obviously express the family's unprocessed dysfunctions, are the ones who are brought to therapy. He aptly called these individuals the "identified patients." It was revolutionary to recognize that the whole family is in need of help and the "identified patient" is just the indicator—a victim not only of the family system but also of a psychological system that labels the individual as the sick one.

When individuals deviate not from the family's but from the *culture's* norms, and are diagnosed and labeled accordingly, the same logic applies. As revisioned activists, we must critically examine the function of psychology as a diagnostic and labeling system. We must inquire about whether those who are diagnosed (whether as addicted, paranoid, bipolar, or borderline) should be lying on the therapeutic couch—or if the client on the couch should be mainstream culture and its values and norms.

Consider the fact that currently, 15 percent of all school-age boys and seven percent of all school-age girls have been diagnosed with attention deficit hyperactivity disorder (ADHD). That means a total of 11 percent of all school-aged children in the United States have been diagnosed with ADHD.[8]

Dr. William Graf, a pediatric neurologist and professor at the Yale School of Medicine, told *The New York Times*, "Mild symptoms are being diagnosed so readily, which goes well beyond the disorder and beyond the zone of ambiguity to pure enhancement of children who are otherwise healthy."[9] And CDC director Dr. Thomas R. Frieden noted in 2013 that "misuse [of ADHD medications] appears to be growing at an alarming rate."[10]

The rapid increase in the number of children taking Ritalin, Adderall, and other ADHD medications has long caused concern among medical professionals, with the harshest critics alleging that children are being drugged to make them easier to teach in the public school system.

Psychology is not being used only to heal the sick, but to make children better performers—or more adapted to teachers' limits of tolerance.

The careful and intelligent diagnosis and treatment of mental illness is a worthy endeavor. For many clients, it's a relief to get diagnosed because it gives them a reason for their suffering, a greater understanding of it, and the sense that they are not alone. However, to make a psychological diagnosis, the psychologist must assess the client's mental, emotional, and behavioral functioning. Because it's difficult (if not impossible) to measure such factors objectively, psychologists often rely on cultural norms to make their diagnoses, labeling individuals who disturb the status quo as "ill." Diagnosing individuals can therefore be an insidious force against cultural diversity.

The power to determine who is psychologically healthy and who is sick must be critically examined and checked. A revisioned activism must focus its lens clearly on psychology's use and abuse of this power.

Marginalization: Psychology's Support of the Individual's Status Quo

While we must ensure that psychology doesn't promote diagnosing or changing people to fit into the culture's status quo, we must also make sure psychology doesn't bias its message and interventions toward preserving the *individual's* status quo—supporting their comfort zone and protecting against deeper change. We therefore need a psychology that doesn't relegate disturbing feelings and impulses to the shadow, where they are out of sight but far from out of mind (pun intended), leading to symptoms that are physical, emotional, and relational without seeming cause to the untrained eye.

Unfortunately, popular psychology often marginalizes disturbing behavior patterns in exactly this way. Self-help books, magazines, blogs, social media memes, and TV ads are constantly bombarding us with the message that we are in need of correction and we should try their methods to rid ourselves of troubling feelings and behavior patterns. We are counseled to stop eating certain foods or ingesting certain substances, as if there were nothing to learn from exploring our yearnings; to stop making certain choices, as if there were no deeper reasons for our actions; to anti-depress, as if emotions that move us into ourselves had nothing to offer us; and to forgive, as if there were nothing of value in our anger.

These quick-fix remedies rarely address the issues underlying our struggles or offer ways to deepen personal transformation in a sustainable way. They are, indeed, shadowless, supporting the individual to restore or strengthen their status quo rather than seek the deeper meaning and more radical changes that their disturbances may call for.

More specifically, when we complain of being depressed, we are often counseled to exercise to raise our energy level; when we are anxious, we are told, "don't worry" or "overcome your fears." And when we are angry, people push on us the medicine of forgiveness and letting go.

Certainly, there are times when this counsel is useful. But more often, these disturbances are better understood as activist impulses that are urging us to make changes in our lives—changes to our status quo. Thus, depression may have a message in it: "My life is empty, unfulfilling." A lack of energy might be a needed correction to a compulsively overproductive, overambitious value system. Worry might be warning us, "This is really scary; stop acting so secure when you don't feel that way." Anger might be telling us, "I'm taking too much crap from people and can't stand up for myself." Psychology, especially popular psychology, has too often acted against these activist messages, suppressing our impulses for inner diversity and working against a more just life.

Further, there is a social cost to this bias against the shadow. If we suppress our anger, we are likely to project our feelings onto others, accusing them of being angry. If we stuff down our depression because we judge ourselves to be lazy, we are likely to project laziness onto others. And these "others" are likely to be people of color, people from religions other than our own, or people who have less money than we do. In short, we can't get away with denying our own shadows without the cost of projection, leading to the stereotyping of target populations in a way that is unmoved by rational logic, but that is supported by a quite intractable "psycho-logic."

Finally, a shadowless psychology extracts a heavy toll from individuals, relationships, and communities. The individual feels shame about what disturbs them, leading them to disengage from relationship and deprive themselves from the community of others who also suffer and are less afraid to be transparent. Suppressing our suffering, our shared humanity, may be the core dysfunction that starves us of our empathy for others and feeds our contempt—and even demonization—of whole groups of people.

In short, when psychology excludes the shadow, it not only works against diversity, it encourages projection onto marginalized others, rendering it complicit in creating social bias. A revisioned activism needs to counter psychology's allopathic bias: its goal of eliminating what people find disturbing.

The renowned African-American scholar and activist Dr. Cornel West aptly declared, "We live in a hotel civilization ... in which people are obsessed with comfort, contentment, and convenience, where the lights are always on."[11] Popular psychology would do well to listen to Dr. West's admonition and learn to follow clients' difficulties into the shadows, into the dark.

Individualization: Psychology's Focus on Individuals

The field of psychology has too often neglected the intersection between individual suffering and social bias. The vast majority of popular psychology and personal growth literature addresses psychological difficulties as if understanding and treatment begins and ends with the individual (and sometimes the family). As I've discussed, when women suffer from self-esteem issues and struggle to stand up for themselves, or when men complain of performance anxiety, these issues are rarely independent of a sexist culture that assigns roles and gives support based on stereotypical gender feelings and behaviors. When our gay sisters and brothers suffer from depression, it would be truly naïve to leave society's heterosexist bias out of our analysis. And when our Jewish friends wrestle with paranoia or concerns about illness, a therapeutic approach that neglects Jewish history can lead Jews to conclude that their suffering is solely a manifestation of their personal problems and pathologies, instead of recognizing that these symptoms are a result of unprocessed Jewish trauma related to the Holocaust.[12]

Imagine, if you will, going to the literature on stress as a black woman and seeing nothing that speaks about racism, historical trauma, or the fact that African-American women tend to age at a faster rate than white women in America. Or imagine being a Native American woman reading a book on stress that fails to mention that the infant mortality rate for Native Americans is 22% higher than that of the general U.S. population.[13]

In essence, many of us seek information about ourselves from sources that fail to connect social status, identity, and marginalization to individual suffering. Histories are whitewashed, and many are presented with a psychology that was formulated without them in mind—a psychology that is complicit in the further internalization of the very forces that are causing our suffering.

To echo the wisdom of Native American psychologists Dr. Karina L. Walters and Dr. Jane M. Simoni, we need models that locate individual suffering "within the larger context of ... colonized people."[14]

Although some specialists, like Walters and Simoni, focus on working with marginalized populations, this perspective is not readily accessible to the vast majority of people who are seeking guidance for personal growth. Perhaps this is one reason why psychology as a tool for healing is less popular with people of color than with white people.

An activist-centered psychology must acknowledge that it has a white mainstream center of gravity, and must accept its mission to truly support a deeper and more whole diversity by waking us all up to the way society, history, and culture contribute to individual suffering.

HOW TO USE THIS BOOK AND WHOM IT IS FOR

We need a revisioned activism: an activism that recognizes moments when our thinking transforms, that broadens current activist efforts, and that opens our eyes to the individual suffering caused by social injustice.

The essays in this book support this thesis but do not further explain it. They are intended for general readers who are interested in personal growth, as well as therapists, psychologists, activists, and teachers and students of sociology and psychology. Topics are wide-ranging, but all of the essays challenge traditional activist assumptions, promoting a revisioned activist approach. The essays are grouped into the following four sections:

- Racism, Anti-Semitism, and Homophobia: Witnessing Social Justice
- Hunger, Self-Hatred, Failure, and Sexism: The Real Weight-Loss Story
- What's Going On? Reflections on Current Events
- Beyond a Popular Psychology: Remembering the Shadow

Section I:
Racism, Anti-Semitism, and Homophobia:
Witnessing Social Justice

Traditional activism rightly raises a battle cry against xenophobia in all its manifestations: homophobia, racism, anti-Semitism, ableism, Islamophobia, and more. However, few psychology writers examine how mainstream ways of thinking sustain and defend these dynamics, how perpetrators are unconsciously motivated by a sense of their own powerlessness, or how marginalized people are among America's greatest teachers of love and democracy.

Traditional activism focuses on what injustice looks like—*what* it is, *where* it exists, and *how much* suffering it causes, from injurious attitudes and language to institutionalized policies and practices. In this section, I focus on a *why:* why we are tethered to these biases and why so many still deny that they exist. I unpack how different groups communicate about injustice, and I offer strategies for improving that communication.

Traditional activism focuses on the horror of slavery and the Holocaust as well as current acts of social injustice, including the decimation of Jewish graves and temples, racist practices built into our criminal justice system, workplace discrimination against LGBTQ people, and the use of hate speech to malign others based on their group identity. But activism must also address our unconscious biases in how we analyze and talk about these events, not simply the bias in the events themselves.

For example, I shine a revisionist light on how mainstream society denies racism by exploring the legacy of Martin Luther King and the racial blindness and projections that have clouded his message. I also focus on the current national call to have a conversation about race. I delve into what it takes for white people to listen deeply to the pain and anger of our African-American brothers and sisters and to engage in a productive, healing dialogue about race.

I explore anti-Semitism in a discussion about how some politicians and pundits have co-opted the terms "Hitler" and "Nazi" to describe almost anybody they don't like, which diminishes and dismisses the anti-Semitism that fueled the Holocaust and the grand scale of that horror. I focus on forms of bias more subtle than the Jewish stereotypes and slurs that are typically given attention.

In this section I also strongly challenge the judgments that straight folks project on gay folks, especially those who are HIV-positive. It broadens the light that other activists shine on more blatantly homophobic actions and policies, all of which carry responsibility for the high suicide rates of LGBTQ youth.

Section II:
Hunger, Self-Hatred, Failure, and Sexism:
The Real Weight-Loss Story

Our country's $60 billion diet industry preys on women who carry tremendous shame about their bodies, literally banking on their suffering and failure.[15] Making matters worse, the solutions it offers work only 5 to 10 percent of the time, amplifying the self-hatred of dieters and turning their hope into one more reason to feel shame.[16]

To talk about weight loss without talking about sexism and the suffering specific to women in our culture is just wrong. To talk about weight loss without talking about how much internalized body hatred women have is just wrong. To promote weight-loss programs and theories without talking about how many thin young girls are dieting is just wrong. To talk about the problems caused by obesity without talking about the problems caused by eating disorders is just wrong. To ignore the high failure rates of diets is to set women up to feel even worse about themselves.

Besides their inherent sexism, discussions and programs about weight loss rarely address the deeper reasons why people eat the way they do. People eat in ways that are physically unhealthy in order to meet valid needs—needs that are most often unconscious, waiting to be discovered. Addressing America's obesity problem by criticizing people's eating and exercising habits—without a deeper understanding of real human needs and the obstacles we face in meeting those needs—is hurtful, not helpful.

In my view, any weight-loss program that doesn't leave a person feeling better about themselves, regardless of whether they do or don't lose weight, is likely to do more long-term harm than good.

In this section, I bring these issues to the surface by citing research and sharing stories from my therapeutic practice working with women clients on their body image issues and weight-loss efforts. These essays are meant to provoke critical thinking about sexism, to challenge the diet industry (which has mostly escaped scrutiny by activists), and to highlight a "love ethic" (in the words of MLK) that contrasts with the belief that criticism is a tool of sustainable change.

These essays are further designed to enlighten men, but especially women, to the social forces at work when they look in the mirror, step on a bathroom scale, and get dressed to meet the world —highlighting these as moments of activism.

Section III:
What's Going On? Reflections on Current Events

"[I]f we were not so single-minded about keeping our lives moving, and for once could do nothing, perhaps a huge silence might interrupt this sadness of never understanding ourselves and of threatening ourselves with death."
—Pablo Neruda

In our workaholic American culture, we pride ourselves on remaining focused on our tasks and goals. But if significant world events don't give us pause and inspire self-reflection, then this single-mindedness becomes a form of denial that our media is too often complicit in.

The media has the power to bring collective awareness to many serious problems, from school shootings to racially charged court trials to the tragedies of suicide and addiction. But as revisioned activists, we must train a critical eye on the culture at large and its complicity in these problems. The media tends to blame the individual and stereotype those with mental health diagnoses, fostering the naïve hope that the world's problems are "out there," divorced from our personal lives. Its rallying cry is more about getting us back to the mall than promoting deeper reflection.

As activists, we must unearth our unconscious assumptions so we can approach these problems armed with more than new regulations, policies, and strategies for policing.

In this section, I expose the cultural meaning that the media neglected in its presentation of the fictions told by news anchor Brian Williams, the death of Phillip Seymour Hoffman by heroin overdose, the trial of George Zimmerman for killing Trayvon Martin, the mass shooting of 20 children in Newtown, and more.

As James Baldwin wrote more than a half-century ago, "[I]t is not permissible that the authors of devastation should also be innocent. It is the innocence which constitutes the crime."[17]

Section IV:
Beyond a Popular Psychology:
Remembering the Shadow

When did psychology become bumper stickers promoting the market values of mainstream success, which urge us to be more functional, energetic, smiling, cooperative, and secure—and less anxious, vulnerable, down, and depressed?

A psychology with no shadow, that fears the darkness and fights to keep us in the light, is an impotent psychology that cannot address society's biggest problems, including war, domestic violence, addiction, self-hatred, racism, and terrorism. It is a psychology that cannot address the harm done when an individual lacks the inner and outer resources to follow the path of their own heart. It is a psychology that follows the path of "a whole century of normative psychology, an approach to mental health that has more to do with socialization than with well-being."[18]

Popular psychology has fallen victim to a craving for quick fixes —affirmations on refrigerator magnets, Internet memes, and shows like *Dr. Phil*. It fails to address our true life project—to be authentic human beings following our own authentic paths. Instead, it tries to help us be more "successful," forgive faster, compromise more readily, anti-depress and anti-grieve, and try conventional weight-loss strategies to feel better about ourselves.

Indeed, psychology has abandoned our souls in its flight to the light, and this serves to keep our culture profoundly deprived of soul food—psychological intelligence, insight, and development.

In this section, I explore how forgiving too readily may invite future injury and suppress our true feelings; how striving for harmony may censor the words and feelings that would lead to more sustainable resolutions; how insisting on color blindness may invalidate the pain of those who don't have the privilege of being treated as colorless; and how the values of productivity and success may reject the qualities of tenderness, sensitivity, and creativity.

With this book, I hope to take you, the reader, on a journey with me beneath the surface, to the place where our shadows live —our own shadows, and those of society. If we can stand still in that place long enough for our fear and aversion to subside, we can begin to listen to those shadows, listen to what they are asking from us. We might hear voices that disturb us, voices of our own diversity, impelling us to change our life course in ways that terrify and excite us to the core. We might realize we could become revisioned activists—and that in so becoming, we could change ourselves and the world.

Racism, Anti-Semitism, and Homophobia: Witnessing Social Justice

The American Soul:
Honoring Our Black Elders

Gurus, yogis, meditation masters, lamas—these are spiritual authorities for many New Age Americans who look to the East for wisdom. But while teachers from Gandhi to the Dalai Lama have shone fine Eastern light to illuminate our paths, this cultural turn to the East can inadvertently dismiss the spiritual wisdom of our own African-American elders—teachings rooted in our own soil, pain, and shadow.

These spiritual teachers are Fanny Lou Hamer and Dr. Martin Luther King, Jr., who faced beating and death with voices compelled by love. They are John Coltrane, whose vision of individual freedom and collective expression manifested in some of America's finest music, as well as Billie Holiday and Nina Simone, who brought soul to pain and misery. (Is there a finer thing for a spiritual tradition to do?)

They are Howard Thurman, who brilliantly guided the practice of a uniquely American Christianity, and Cornel West, whose intellect and spirit soar in pronouncement of a love-based ethic. And how could we leave out Toni Morrison and Maya Angelou, African-American women who have revealed the glory and redemption we need as individuals and as a nation. These teachers don't turn water into wine; they turn tears into the blues. They don't walk on water;

they create music that we float on. They don't carry a staff and part the Red Sea, but they do honor to the Hebrew cry, "Let my people go."

These elders, and countless others, have elucidated a spiritual wisdom that was born in the fires of America's own alchemy, through a process of cooking the demons and injuries of injustice along with the spirit of love and perseverance into a unique brilliance. Their wisdom honors and redeems those who have bled for America's soul.

To many, these individuals may not look like spiritual teachers —but not because they lack spiritual riches to offer. I remember wondering why I was listening to Buddhist chanting instead of John Coltrane's "Love Supreme" during my morning meditation period. I remember several black elders teaching me how to make heated dialogue into a meditation on relationship instead of an inner practice of loving-kindness. I remember Dr. King waking me up to the fact that spirituality is also a public practice when I heard him say that "justice is what love looks like in public." I recall Maya Angelou teaching me how to turn great suffering into powerful humanity, a practice I had previously sought in Eastern teachings. I recall poet Etheridge Knight singing to me of desperation, imprisonment, and freedom, lessons that Eastern spiritual teachers had taught me years before.

Of course, these black teachers don't don robes, hold weekend workshops, or show up in the kind of classrooms or retreat centers that many associate with spiritual teaching. Most Americans would liken these elders to artists and activists more than spiritual teachers. And sitting at the feet of these elders challenges our fundamental paradigm of education, especially spiritual education. Nonetheless, their spiritual powers cannot be denied. They offer a way of living, loving, and dying in a world of darkness as well as light.

To be clear, I have no inherent objection to Eastern philosophies and spiritual disciplines. I have been a student of many fine minds and hearts, from Sharon Salzberg and Pema Chödrön to

Bhante Gunaratana, Stephen Levine, and Jack Kornfield, teachers who helped bring Eastern traditions to the United States. But when these teachings are highlighted at the expense of teachings forged on the backs of those who have suffered under the weight of America's shadow, an injustice is perpetrated. For the purpose of righting this injustice, I offer the following critique of some Eastern and New Age teachings in contrast to the relative value and power of African-American wisdom teachings for all Americans today.

First, some New Age and Eastern teachings foster practices that avoid the shadow. Practitioners often attempt to relieve pain and suffering rather than investigating its meaning; they seek bliss even when their path is taking them into their deeper feelings; they can be found blessing each other while remaining unconscious of how they patronize. I have witnessed groups of such practitioners being open-hearted toward streaming tears but *not* toward screaming ire. I have seen competition and jealousy treated as negatives to be rooted out *instead of as fire and heat to deepen the knowledge of self and the bonds of community.* At its worst, this kind of spirituality can become a form of denial, a flight toward spirit that denies the soul's descent, risking the same fire that brought Icarus back to earth.

In contrast, much African-American teaching is rooted in shadow. Its elders have sat in the fire of brutality as well as in projections of inferiority, aggression, and deviance. I am reminded of an African-American man who attended a workshop on conflict resolution with some 300 participants from over 25 different countries. Many of us grew to admire his wisdom, personal power, and leadership capacity when he helped to resolve our most protracted tensions. He had a hard-earned ease with anger and aggression that most of us didn't. One night he walked into our workshop hall pushing a mop and garbage pail and singing a song from slavery times. He said that in his garbage pail was all that we throw away —aspects of our sexuality, our greed, our anger, our desperation, and more. "I eat this garbage," he said. "I live on all that you throw away, and that's what makes me strong, true, and a person you look to for keys on how to be alive." His spirit had grown strong in the shadow of mainstream America's compulsion to climb the ladder of success and higher states of consciousness, leaving behind the rags and bones of a true spirituality.

Second, practitioners of New Age and Eastern traditions often urge individuals to handle disturbing feelings like hurt, anger, insecurity, and impatience by looking inside themselves. Many use these same practices as a way of avoiding relationship difficulties and conflict. When the practitioner is angry with their partner, they may turn to their meditation cushion instead of learning to address the issues directly. When they have judgments about their families and communities, many practice letting go of these feelings rather than using the power and impulse of their judgments to speak out for change and healing.

In contrast, through music, protest, and the church's call and response, African-American elders teach dialogue and the fine art of democracy. Like the conversation between voices and instruments in jazz music, this dialogue makes beauty and moral/spiritual development out of engaged interaction, even when it is heated.

Third, some practitioners of New Age spirituality promote the concept that we choose our reality, our emotions, and what comes into our lives. But this perspective can inadvertently deny the genuine victimization and collective responsibility for injustice perpetrated against groups—from blacks and women to Jews and gays —by suggesting that all responsibility lies with the individual's consciousness and not with the collective unconscious. It is worth noting that this kind of denial is less likely to be promoted by people who are marginalized by mainstream culture, *people who are more likely to be treated as members of a group rather than as individuals*. A friend recently quoted an Eastern spiritual teacher as saying that working on our own individual consciousness is the most important thing we do. I responded that I had a slight allergy to spiritual ideas that highlight the consciousness of the individual over that of the collective.

In contrast, I am reminded of Emmett Till's mother, who said in front of the open casket of her murdered son, "I've not a minute to waste; I will pursue justice for the rest of my life."[1] She practiced a spirituality aimed at awakening a whole culture and freeing their hearts and souls regardless of their personal choices or practices.

Finally, while many who turn to the East consider themselves to be progressive, their progressive attitudes often manifest in condescension, caretaking, and charity towards blacks and other marginalized groups. While they may be involved in working toward social justice, they don't treat our African-American wise women and men with the same authority, respect, and reverence they do their Eastern spiritual teachers, whose feet they are more likely to sit at.

In contrast, some of our African-American teachers once sat at the feet of those who spoke for America's Judeo-Christian heritage. I am reminded of the slave woman who, on her knees, prayed to God to forgive her Christian slave owner, who stood above her, believing he was spiritually superior. She prayed, "Oh Lord, bless my master. When he calls upon thee to damn his soul, do not hear him, do not hear him, but hear me—save him—make him know he is wicked, and he will pray for thee."[2] She who was on her knees was the teacher; he who stood above was in need of redemption. Is this not the kind of reversal as well as and spiritual/moral education Americans still need today?

As an ethnic Jew, I am aware of how African-Americans have enriched the story of Moses. Zora Neal Hurston's novel *Moses, Man of the Mountain* presaged the Civil Rights Movement, and civil rights activists embodied the great prophet's story of freedom. This poetic irony highlights the depth of a people who were often more spiritually developed while assuming a station of inferiority.

The poet Rainer Maria Rilke suggested, almost one hundred years ago, that people in the West suffer a kind of soullessness and have lost their spiritual way. As a result, their children may need to go far out into the East, "towards that same church which [they] forgot."[3] Rilke's words were prophetic—a whole generation did indeed go far to the East to find their "church" unconsciously turning a blind eye to their African-American elders.

Why look to the East? Why not sit at the feet of America's African-American wisdom teachers? Let me suggest that reaching out to this tradition, especially as white folks, means bearing a certain pain and, yes, responsibility for a legacy of suffering. In this way, many of us don't walk into this "church" with clean hands—a pain we need not face in the ashram or zendo. However, bearing this pain may be just the deepening we need.

The "color line," in the words of W. E. B. Du Bois, still demarcates social boundaries.[4] And while many of us have joined our voices with those who call for social justice, this attitude doesn't embody the same valuation as looking up to folks for spiritual wisdom and development.

James Baldwin wrote, "The black man has functioned in the white man's world as a fixed star, as an immovable pillar, and as he moves out of his place, heaven and earth are shaken to their foundations."[5] It's time to shake our foundations, root out our negative projections and stereotypes, and end the unconscious devaluation and patronization of America's black elders. While much wisdom can be found in Eastern New Age traditions, there is a rich tradition of wisdom grown right here, paid for in blood and tears, and ready-made to speak to the souls and psyches of Americans today.

2

MLK Today:
Taking the Blinders off White Privilege

H ow far have we really come since Dr. King's passing in 1968? Could those who argue that we now live in a truly post-racial society be wearing the blinders of white privilege? Consider the following.

Have we achieved Dr. King's goal of eradicating racial prejudice?

Some would surely say yes. Recently I dined at a fairly pricey French restaurant, where I had a conversation with the white woman at the table next to mine. She and her husband lived in Manhattan's Upper East Side and also had a vacation home in Santa Fe, New Mexico, where I currently live. I grew up in New York City; that was our common ground. We got on the topic of the choking death of Eric Garner and the protests in its wake.

She said, "Before Mayor de Blasio spoke up in support of the black protests, there weren't really any racial issues in New York. We had gotten past that."

"That's simply not true," I retorted. "The racial tension had been there all the time. [Mayor] de Blasio didn't create it. Many folks, especially black folks, knew it was there all the time."

From where did this woman derive her perception? I don't think she was mean-spirited; in many ways, she was quite intelligent. However, a certain psychological intelligence was absent—the ability to realize that her framework was her experience as a wealthy white person.

She had the unearned privilege of never being disadvantaged by racial stereotypes. She had the privilege of not needing to listen to and feel the pain of black New Yorkers, many of whom have stories and perspectives that clearly wouldn't match her own. She had the privilege of needing neither data nor experience to feel free to issue her definitive opinion.

In short, she drew on her unconscious privilege to conclude that racial prejudice was a thing of the past.

Is "color blindness" the key to being judged by the content of our character?

Many argue, "If color blindness was good enough for Martin Luther King, then it ought to be good enough for a society that still aspires to the movement's goals of equality and fair treatment."[1]

Much of the argument for color blindness relies on a superficial reading of Dr. King's "I Have a Dream" speech, when he said, "I have a dream that my four little children will one day live in a nation where they will not be judged by the color of their skin but by the content of their character." Based on this statement, some argue that Dr. King believed racism would be ended when Americans no longer saw race.

What allows many folks, especially white folks, to maintain this belief? I know of no data to support the notion that this kind of color blindness helps alleviate racial disparities or racial injustice. In my experience, many who espouse this view simply have no idea what it is like to live in a dark-skinned body. They have the unearned privilege of not having to think of themselves racially.

Dr. Beverly Tatum, former psychology professor and current president of Spellman College, used to regularly conduct an experiment with her psychology students. She asked them to complete the sentence, "I am _____."[2] She found that while students of color typically mentioned their racial identity, white students rarely mentioned being white. The same was true for gender; women were more likely to mention being female. She concluded that racial identity for white folks is not reflected back to them and thus remains somewhat unconscious.

In short, black folks simply don't have the privilege of not seeing themselves as a color, and they know others will see them as such, whereas many white folks easily enjoy not seeing their own color. Trying to not see race before we are truly awake to racism's ugly present and past assigns racism to our individual and collective shadow, rendering its harm more insidious because it hides in seeming good-heartedness and innocence.

To quote Dr. King, "Nothing in the world is more dangerous than sincere ignorance and conscientious stupidity."[3]

Is affirmative action contrary to Dr. King's dream of not being judged by the color of our skin?

I recently dialogued with a white man who insisted that Dr. King was opposed to affirmative action. He was immune to my presentation of Dr. King's views from my extensive reading on the issue. Instead, he said, "I choose to take Dr. King at his word; the man was quite articulate and capable of saying what he meant." Again, he referred to Dr. King's "Dream" speech. He continued, "It seems pretty clear that for members of any race to expect preferential treatment because of their race is unacceptable. It doesn't matter how noble one's motives. It's wrong."

What was wrong was his reading of Dr. King. In his 1964 book *Why We Can't Wait*, King wrote, "Whenever the issue of compensatory treatment for the Negro is raised, some of our friends recoil in horror. The Negro should be granted equality, they agree; but he should ask nothing more."[4] Later, in 1967, he wrote, "A society that has done something special against the Negro for hundreds of years must now do something special for him."[5]

However, we must not stop there. Again we must ask: Why was it so easy for this white man, despite my argument about King's actual words, to maintain his position? While I confess to not knowing this man's mind and heart, many white folks I have dialogued with are unaware of the preferential treatment they receive —that they are the beneficiaries of the affirming actions of a racially biased society—while black folks are still the beneficiaries of disconfirming actions.

For example, when blacks apply for a job, they are less likely to get selected than whites (even if the applications are identical in every other way).[6] White folks get "extra points," a kind of affirmative action.

Black folks are more likely to get stopped and frisked than white folks, even when what they are carrying is identical.[7] That's a kind of affirming action for whites.

Black folks are up to three times more likely to get the death sentence than whites in similar cases.[8] I could go on about differential school funding, bank lending practices, and more. The truth is that white folks, in general, receive perhaps less overt but quite real and potent benefits that black folks do not.

When a person swims in an ocean of relative affirmation, it is almost natural to be unconscious of the fact that their achievements, confidence, and successes are not only a result of their own capacity and efforts. Unconsciousness of these privileges makes it easy to conclude that a more overt policy of affirmative action is a form of preferential treatment to black folks instead of a leveling of the playing field.

If we are to enrich the national dialogue about race, if we are to make further progress toward Dr. King's dream, our collective awareness of unconscious privilege must grow. Then we may find what Langston Hughes exhorted us to wake up to:

That Justice is a blind goddess

Is a thing to which we black are wise:

Her bandage hides two festering sores

That once perhaps were eyes.[9]

3

Dreaming King's Dream Forward: Reflections on America's Psyche

Many fine essays and books have been written about Dr. Martin Luther King, Jr., detailing his impact on American life, law, and culture. But few focus on the American psyche—how we see, or don't see, Dr. King. Consider these six ways Americans bear witness to Dr. King and his legacy, each involving conflicting points of view.

1. Hero or idol?

Many Americans view Dr. King as a hero, and it's natural to admire heroes. However, when a hero becomes a projection—an object instead of a subject—they become idolized. We see only the best in these people; we believe our own failings make us less worthy than they are; and we deprive our heroes of their humanity, their pain, their loneliness, their need.

Like Dr. King, Mother Teresa was a hero to many, which is why a posthumously published book of her correspondence was so startling. It revealed that for the last almost fifty years of her life she felt no presence of God. David Van Biema wrote in *Time Magazine*: "*Come Be My Light* is that rare thing, a posthumous autobiography that could cause a wholesale reconsideration of a major public figure."[1] Some might conclude that Mother Teresa was a hypocrite, but many readers were touched deeply, related to her doubt and loneliness, saw her as human, and felt that their own paths were validated.

The Caribbean-American writer and scholar June Jordan spoke in perhaps an equally startling way about Dr. King, saying, "He made big mistakes ... He did not abstain from whiskey, tobacco, or sex ... He committed adultery ... He did like him a little sugar in his bowl."[2] "But seeing King in his wholeness," she later adds, "I have come to praise him, and to try to follow after Martin Luther King, Jr., this Black man of God."[3] Jordan saw the hero, not the idol.

We can idolize the projection of Dr. King. We can love the real person—and ourselves.

2. A dream or a nightmare?

Children wake their parents in the night, saying, "I had a bad dream." Their parents respond, lovingly, "Go back to sleep; it was just a dream." But there is a psychic and social cost if we go back to sleep —if we don't face our shadow as a culture—especially when that shadow is grave social injustice. If we don't grapple with this shadow, our moral conscience is not strengthened by the heat of opposition, and our ethics devolve from cultivated compassion into rules.

Every year on Martin Luther King Jr. Day, Dr. King's "I Have a Dream" speech reverberates over radio airwaves and in the American psyche. "I say to you today, my friends, even though we face the difficulties of today and tomorrow, I still have a dream."[4]

But, as professor and author Michael Eric Dyson notes, we rarely hear another important speech that Dr. King made almost four years later: "In 1963 ... I tried to talk to the nation about a dream that I had had, and I must confess to you today that not long after talking about that dream I started seeing it turn into a nightmare."[5] In fact, Dyson suggests a 10-year moratorium on the "I Have a Dream" speech, an intervention that just might compensate for our predisposition to romanticize, and thus disempower, the real Dr. King.[6]

Dr. King wrote, "The strong man holds in a living blend strongly marked by opposites."[7] Let us hold Dr. King's words about both the dream and the nightmare, so that we may grow stronger and truer as a nation.

3. Highlighting segregation or ending segregation?

According to the Library of Congress, Dr. King "never got tired of trying to end segregation laws ... He also did all he could to make people realize that 'all men are created equal.'"[8] Clearly, neglecting Dr. King's role in confronting segregation would be a serious error. However, preeminent scholar on race and poverty Jonathan Kozol has noted, "America's public schools are more segregated today than they were when Dr. King was assassinated in 1968."[9]

Again, Americans must grapple with two conflicting visions of Dr. King's impact: Great power and change grew out of the Civil Rights Movement he led, as well as great frustration and failure to make certain strides. As the great African-American scholar Cornel West says about this tension, "I'm full of hope but in no way optimistic."[10]

4. Republican or democrat?

Everyone wants a piece of Dr. King. Frances Rice, chairman of the National Black Republican Association, wrote, "Dr. King ... was guided by his faith and his Republican Party principles. ... He did not embrace the type of socialist, secularist agenda that is promoted by the Democrat Party today."[11] Cambridge University historian David

Garrow writes, "King was not only not a Republican, he was well to the left of the Democratic Party of the 1960s."[12]

Psychologically speaking, Dr. King's name often is used to bolster the moral authority of people who fear they do not have it. ("Dr. King was on my side;" "No, Dr. King would have been on my side.") In my years of facilitating conflict, I have seen plainly how people rely on the name and authority of another when they can't quite speak for themselves—their own passion, vision, hearts. In the long run, as opponents felt more empowered to speak their own truths, conflicts were far more likely to resolve. Why? Because many people engage in conflict not so they can be right—but to find the power of their own voice and speak their own truth. To further our democratic experiment, we all need to learn to find and use our voices and not only rely on the voices of others.

5. Color blindness or color denial?

Conversations about color blindness, including debates on affirmative action, often invoke Dr. King's famous statement, "I have a dream that my four little children will one day live in a nation where they will not be judged by the color of their skin but by the content of their character."[13] For example, in his 1992 book *Paved with Good Intentions*, Jared Taylor referred to this speech to make the case that advocating race consciousness, especially by African Americans, "was a rejection ... of the color-blind vision of Martin Luther King."[14] However, in the *New York Law Review*, Jerome McCristal Culp, Jr., wrote in opposition to this kind of thinking: "People have created a mythic Martin Luther King, Jr., and associated him with a fictional notion of color blindness ... created to help us get over the difficulty of race in a society where race is particularly powerful."[15]

While I agree that some use King's words about color blindness to blind them to real issues of race, this debate often ignores a more fundamental psychological principal: When a white person tells a black person that skin color shouldn't be considered, it's different than when a black person tells a white person that skin color shouldn't be considered. (The same is true for all dichotomies where power differences lurk in the background.) The essential difference is not only a logical one—it is also a reflection of two different viewpoints that result from the greater privilege of most white folks compared to that of most black folks. In short, black folks rarely have the privilege of not seeing themselves, or not being seen as, a color.

The issue of color blindness cannot be fully addressed by the kind of logic that neglects the psychology of privilege. If we are to deepen the conversation about race, we must become more conscious of the way privilege affects people's perspectives.

6. Shall we resolve our differences about Dr. King via strong debate or compromise?

How do we perfect our union, further our living democracy? We live in a time of polarization on countless difficult issues; compromise is an endangered species. This polarization was illustrated on August 28, 2010, the forty-seventh anniversary of Dr. King's "I Have a Dream" speech. Conservative pundit Glenn Beck held the Restoring Honor rally, which distorted the history of the Civil Rights Movement, while not far away, civil rights activist Al Sharpton held the Reclaim the Dream rally.

How shall we forge democratic empowerment out of this kind of disparity? Some will counsel seeking common ground so that a form of compromise can be achieved. Others will stand firm in their position, citing authorities, facts, or data. However, while both of these approaches are needed, neither will bring us to a deep and sustainable resolution.

While seeking resolution may be motivated by a dream of truth, harmony, or even justice, it can easily come at the cost of marginalizing the very diversity and differences that are the fundamental building blocks, the DNA, of our unfolding democracy. Al Sharpton and Glenn Beck each represent the voices of many. *Beneath the content of their arguments, they channel a frustration, an insufficiently considered pain, and an urge for justice.* In this way, together, Sharpton and Beck further the unfolding of our democracy, King's dream of a "beloved community."

Dr. Martin Luther King, Jr. was a man of God, to be sure, whose life changed the landscape of America and her budding democracy. But he also lives vibrantly in the American psyche, as demonstrated in how we refer to him, use his words, argue his position, and reflect on his legacy. It is my dream that understanding how we dream of Dr. King will nourish the soul of our country and this beloved community.

4

What's the Matter with "All Lives Matter"?

In 2012, George Zimmerman, a white neighborhood watchman, shot and killed Trayvon Martin, an unarmed black teenager. Zimmerman was charged, tried, and ultimately acquitted. In the aftermath of his acquittal, the grassroots movement Black Lives Matter was born.[1]

Black Lives Matter focuses on the disproportionate level of police violence against black people in the United States. It also works to broaden the conversation around race to include the burdens on black women, children, black queer and trans folks, and blacks with disabilities.

In response, some white folks have countered with the slogan, "All lives matter." While this phrase may at first glance seem to be even more empowering and diversity-affirming, it is neither.

In the shadow of "All lives matter" lurks a form of willful color blindness — of erasing the issue of race.

When people say "All lives matter" in response to Black Lives Matter, they are not opening their arms to the greater diversity of humanity. Rather, they are trying to take race out of the conversation. While the statement masquerades as a bright and inclusive light, in its shadow hides a deliberate ignorance of America's racist past and present.

There is no doubt that racism exists today. The evidence is vast, clear, and widely available. Just look at differential statistics for stop-and-frisk rates,[2] sentencing levels,[3] and job hiring.[4]

A most telling data point about the difference in our valuation of a black life comes from a study conducted by Allan Collard-Wexler, an economist at NYU Stern School of Business: In order to make parents indifferent to race, the cost of adopting a black baby must be $38,000 lower than the cost of a white baby.[5]

Adding insult to injury, "All lives matter" is a form of dismissing and denying America's racist past.

Through the institution of slavery, the wording of the U.S. Constitution, and Jim Crow laws, the U.S. government upheld the belief that some lives were more human, more worthy—that some lives mattered more. How can we forget that America codified in its Constitution (the same Constitution that some insist must be strictly and literally interpreted in its original form) the notion that a black life was considered to be only three-fifths of a white life?

If we stop focusing on black lives, but instead focus more globally and generally on all lives, then we become complicit in not seeing color as an important factor in American social dynamics. *Putting it simply, if we erase race, we won't have to look at racism.*

In the shadow of "All lives matter" lurks the privilege white folks have to avoid experiencing their own lives in racial terms.

Let's face it, most white people don't regularly think about themselves as white. We are not made to think about our race, because we are not living in an environment that injures white people because of our skin color. Therefore, we easily think of ourselves as a "just a person," as a human being belonging to the human family.

But when a person is regularly injured because of a certain quality, it is virtually impossible to enjoy the luxury of ignoring that quality. My Eastern European brothers and sisters could not ignore the fact that they were Jewish. (If they "forgot," they were quickly reminded!) Women in boardrooms, disabled people getting on a bus, gay youth at a high school dance, and black teens in a school cafeteria are all aware of their social identity. Straight, white, able-bodied males ignore their social identity.[6] They enjoy the privilege of being free from that concern. (For more on this topic, I recommend Beverly Daniel Tatum's *Why Are All the Black Kids Sitting Together in the Cafeteria?*)[7]

When a white person counters the statement "Black lives matter" with "All lives matter," they reveal a blindness to their privilege—the privilege of living outside the lens that highlights and marginalizes people because of the color of their skin.

In the words of writer Jarune Uwujaren, "[I]f you have trouble seeing race or are tired of people making things about race, realize that if they could, most people of color would ignore race too."[8]

In the shadow of "All lives matter" is an aggressive resistance to focusing on the value of black lives.

The slogan "All lives matter" did not arise in a vacuum. It was not born of a passion for the value of all beings, including black beings. It is not a worldwide social movement for justice. It was a rebuttal, a retort, a counterpoint to the statement "Black lives matter." While not everyone utters these words with this intent, the phrase nonetheless functions as a dismissal.

Instead of communicating a reverence for life, "All lives matter" are words of negation, repudiation, and refutation. They are fighting words. Fighting what? Simple: That black lives matter!

On a personal note, beyond all logical argument, I confess to having tears flow when I first visited the Black Lives Matter website and found recorded black voices completing the phrase, "In a world where black lives matter, I imagine...." One recording was made by Satchel, a four-year-old black boy, who erupted in sweet giggling joy after saying, "In a world where black lives matter, I imagine ... there's a lot of tickling."[9]

In a world that would resist or belittle the declaration that black lives matter—that would censor those who speak out for the beauty, power, intelligence, and moral authority of black people—I fear there would be far fewer black children smiling, laughing, and giggling, and far more hungering for food, safety, and a sense of self-worth.

5

America's Deadly Denial of Racism

In April 2015, Walter Scott, an unarmed black man, was shot five times while running away from Michael Slager, a white police officer.[1] Slager was arrested and charged with murder. Articles and news reports have focused on this incident as the act of one white officer, urging us to think that this time, justice may be served.

A month before that shooting, four Florida police officers were found to be exchanging texts and videos with KKK hoods on the topic of "killing n*****s." One texted, "I had a wet dream that you two found those n*****s in the VW and gave them the death penalty right there on the spot." Another wrote, "We are coming and drinking all your beer and killing n*****s." These messages and more were uncovered during a five-month investigation. The result: Three officers were fired, one resigned.[2]

As much as it serves justice that these officers were held to some level of accountability, it is also true that many officers know of their peers' bigotry and do nothing about it. The problem is not only the racism of individual officers; the problem is also systemic. The situation is akin to the sexual abuses discovered within the Catholic Church: There were offending clergymen, and there was also a system that was complicit in keeping the abuses in the shadows and protecting the perpetrators, thus ensuring further victimization.

Racism: Americans' Complicity, Denial, and Naïveté

American psychology—by which I mean the way Americans think about ourselves and our collective social dilemmas—is often painfully naïve. We are like children who believe in the bogeyman and in narratives where the good guys get the bad guys.

However, regarding race, and many other intractable problems of our society (e.g., addiction, depression, domestic violence), getting the bad guys is wholly insufficient. The truth is that *we are the system.* We are all complicit, and we all carry a certain responsibility for racism, America's original sin.

Don't get me wrong—there are bad guys. But it is also our psychological naïveté, our cultural blinders, that allow complicity to spread unchecked. Our denial of racism is a form of racism in and of itself.

Where is this denial evident? Consider these statistics:

- A majority of whites believe that blacks earn as much money as whites. In reality, the median income among black Americans is roughly half that of white Americans.[3]
- Whites believe that over 40% of violent crime is committed by blacks, when it's actually around 20%.[4]
- Black folks in Ferguson are 2.07 times more likely than white folks to be searched during a vehicular stop but are 26% less likely to have contraband found on them during a search.[5]
- A study conducted at the University of Chicago Graduate School of Business found that identical resumes with the names Emily or Brendan are 50% more likely to get called for an initial interview than applicants with the names Lakisha and Jamal. Still, many whites think that blacks have equal opportunity.[6]

It is this denial that leads many white folks to believe that black folks are being arrested and incarcerated because they are more prone to criminality—not because our criminal justice system targets black folks. It is this denial that leads many white folks to believe that black folks take unfair advantage of social services. They don't see that the job market treats black folks unfairly. It is this kind of denial that leads many white folks to malign black leaders, accusing them of "playing the race card" instead of hearing their legitimate claims to injustice.

To honestly confront the psychological illness of racism, America needs a true mirror, one that reflects our light and our shadow, one that provokes a real moral and spiritual awakening. Only then can we bear the truth of our collective responsibility. Only then will we go beyond investigating racist police officers to investigating a system that allows, even supports, the flourishing of racist attitudes and practices.

Only then will we come to the wisdom expressed in Walt Kelly's famous cartoon: "We have met the enemy, and he is us."

6

How to Have a Conversation About Race

The killing of Michael Brown, an 18-year-old black man, by Darren Wilson, a white police officer, on August 9, 2014, has unearthed, yet again, a crisis, a trauma, and a wound in the soul of our nation. The consensus is: have a conversation about race. Sounds clear; feels right (though it is not sufficient when black souls and bodies fall dead to the ground). Why is this conversation so difficult? Is there anything we can do to make it more healing and less likely to cause further injury? I think so; I truly hope so. Here are four suggestions about how to have a conversation about race.

Talk About the Definition of Racism

There is confusion and genuine diversity about how to define the term "racism." Some people use the term to describe any racial bias, regardless of who is the perpetrator and who is the victim. Others reserve the term for white-on-black racial bias only. This difference creates an underlying conflict that prevents the more obvious conflict (e.g., was Officer Wilson racist?) from getting very far or finding a measure of resolution to the deeper racial divide.

The rationale behind labeling all racial bias "racism" is compelling in that it is seemingly logical and fair-minded. However, the reason for applying the term to only white-on-black racial bias is more difficult to understand for many white folks, and elucidating those reasons is critical to having a productive dialogue.

The key issue here is that white-on-black racism is not equivalent to black-on-white racism. Two differences make this true. First, white racial bias has been institutionalized; black racial bias has not. That means that white racial bias is empowered by one person's bias toward another (e.g., one white police officer's bias toward one black male) as well as deeply held beliefs and practices that manifest in the economic system (e.g., in banking practices), the law enforcement system (e.g., in stop-and-frisk practices, incarceration levels), the educational system (e.g., the level of funding of inner-city black schools vs. suburban white schools), the media (e.g., how it presents and stereotypes black folks), and the minds of the general public, who carry mostly unconscious biases (e.g., fears, stereotypes, and projections). This institutionalization amplifies the power of an individual's or group's bias, supercharging it. It is as if two similarly sized people exchanged punches, but one person's punch was made many times more powerful by an invisible force. Many believe there is a kind of equivalence between the punches because they don't see the extra power that one has.

Second, adding to the first, is the fact that white bias against blacks has been a fact for hundreds of years of history, leaving massive injury and trauma in its wake. In this way, the two people in my "punching" example come to the situation very different. One comes remembering past abuse and is already bruised and vulnerable. This makes the punch feel much more injurious, causing much bigger injury and more painful symptoms. Again, many whites don't see this extra vulnerability.

What can we do?

Have a dialogue about the meaning of "racism." Help individuals speak for and support their definition. Do not try to get everyone to agree, especially if the disagreement is strong. Make sure the differences between the racial biases are discussed. Consider this discussion so important and fundamental that it is worth the time of the individuals and group, even if they never get to other issues, like the details of what happened in Ferguson.

Avoid the Bias for a Harmonious or Comfortable Dialogue

Most people prefer conversations that are calm, harmonious, and understanding as opposed to argumentative, judgmental, angry, and aggressive.

However, trying to make conversations about race more harmonious or peaceful often suppresses the deeper feelings and reactions of all parties, especially black folks who are still waiting to be fully heard—a fact that escalates conflict. Judging individuals or the group for being too aggressive, loud, or forceful often escalates strong feelings about the issue. For many black folks, it is equivalent to being told, "You must work to make me comfortable if you want me to listen to you." This can be infuriating for black folks who have been uncomfortable for a long time and are now being told they must make white folks feel comfortable.

Further, this message communicates the assumption that a calmer, harmonious style is a better, more noble one. This too can escalate the conflict because it unintentionally suggests a moral or psychological superiority, which amounts to pouring salt in the wound of history's supremacist attitude and practices.

What can we do?

Before beginning to dialogue about the specific issues on the agenda (e.g., affirmative action, Ferguson, police practices), ask people to share how open they are to various levels of emotion, from anger to tears. This makes the issue of emotional expression more conscious for the group, so people can avoid unintentionally hurting each other.

Don't Let the Notions That "We Are All One and the Same," or That Skin Color Should Not Be an Issue, Suppress Wrestling with Difference

Moments of "race blindness" and connecting to our underlying common humanity are wonderful and carry a level of truth that can be healing for people and groups. However, when conflict about race is present, asserting this "truth" suppresses another truth that is critical to the dialogue: that people have been and still are treated differently based on their skin color. In this way, many black folks don't have the privilege of acting as if race doesn't matter, whereas a white person is more likely to have that privilege.

For example, when a black person accuses me of racism, I don't say that we are both really the same and that I treat all people the same, independent of skin color. That's not the social truth that the person is referring to. To declare or assert that truth would be not to hear that person—their truth, their experience, the empirical fact of the social reality, and what they have to teach me. However, at a moment later in the dialogue, we may be able to touch on and connect to our background commonness and humanity. Both truths are worthy; it's an issue of sensitivity and timing.

What can we do?

Toward the beginning of the dialogue, agree to focus on people's experiences of being black and being white and the differences between these experiences. In addition, some education about privilege can be helpful. Remember that if the truth of our sameness is asserted too early in the discussion, it serves to suppress the very differences that make the dialogue so important and potentially healing in the first place.

Clarify the Level of the Dialogue

There are different levels in conversations about race. The personal or individual level operates when one person is talking to another about their own experience or when people are discussing an incident involving two individuals. For instance, people may speak about Michael Brown as an individual (his motives, body size, state of mind, and intent) or about Officer Wilson (his motives, state of mind, size, and intent). The legal system attempts to operate at this level.

However, many discussions about race exist at another level—a group or social level—where individuals are being felt as and referred to as representatives of a group. At this level, people who speak about Michael Brown are not speaking only about Michael Brown. Instead, they may be talking about black male youth or the history of bias towards black folks over time. And folks who are talking about Officer Wilson may be referring to him as a white police officer and agent of a racially biased law enforcement system, not only about his actions as a particular person. At this level, both individuals become symbols of a larger social dynamic. When these levels are confused, conflict will be unproductive because some people will be talking about an individual bias and some of a generalized systematic bias.

Many people are more comfortable talking at the personal or individual level. We are trained to think this way and hold individuals accountable for their actions. However, focusing only on the individual level will not take into account the larger context and history of bias, which are critical elements of the conflict. On the group level, determining whether Officer Wilson is racist or not, or is guilty of murdering Michael Brown or not, is less important to the discussion. Officer Wilson is functioning as an agent, an expression, of a law enforcement system that has a terrible history and present of racial bias. Wilson can defend himself individually; in a court of law, that's all he is required to do. But in the social context, the public court, he must stand as an agent of the group he represents. This is a very tall order for most of us because we want to be seen as individuals and not take on responsibility for the groups we belong to.

For Wilson to do this, he will have to wear the badge of racism for the purposes of public discourse, because he is empowered with weapons, rights, freedoms, powers, and privileges as a representative of a system that has systemic biases against black folks. Similarly, Michael Brown is not just himself, for the purposes of the discourse; he is one of thousands of dead young black boys and men. Some folks will want to focus only on Michael Brown's culpability or his character in the incident, making it difficult to focus the conversation on the generalized experience of black male youths. Attempting to focus only on the individual level may dissipate the energy of the conflict in the short term. But in the long term, it will inhibit finding more sustainable resolutions and understanding.

What can we do?

When conflicts arise around race, clarify which level is being spoken about as the dialogue proceeds. If this doesn't happen, some people will be referring to what is in Officer Wilson's or Michael Brown's heart or mind, and some will be referring to their social "roles." In addition, when conflicts get hot, try to get the group of people dialoguing to focus on the second level—that of the social roles they represent—because this conflict contains more underlying heat as a result of the history that informs it.

The Holocaust and the Inner Ghetto: The Psychology of Jewish Suffering

According to a 2013 article in the *New York Times*, the number of Nazi concentration camps and ghettos were more than previously imagined—42,500![1] However, not only are we still becoming aware of the literal facts; we are still becoming aware of the psychological facts as well.

Not only did the Holocaust impact the lives of countless people across the world, but it also left specific echoes that still reverberate in the minds, bodies, and psyches of Jews today. For this reason, references to the Holocaust should be made with care for the accuracy of this history and with sensitivity toward the Jewish people.

In today's political discourse, pundits and commentators do not respect this sensitivity. They use the terms "Holocaust" and "Nazi" and invoke the name "Hitler" whenever they want to brand their opponent as evil and incite the wrath of their allies—at the expense of any further dialogue or critical examination of the ideas that offend them. For example, conservative pundits have announced that "liberals are the new Nazis;"[2] that Obama's gun-control proposal will be "like Nazi Germany;"[3] and that Obama playing golf with Speaker Boehner is like "Hitler playing golf with Netanyahu."[4]

It's not only right-wing enthusiasts who step on the sacred gravestones of Nazi victims; left-wing enthusiasts do the same.

Democratic politicians have likened Governor Nikki Haley to Eva Braun[5] and called Paul Ryan's National Convention speech "Nazi propaganda."[6] Actually, the offenders reach way beyond our political rhetoric and are too numerous to list here.

There are three problems with the unconscious and casual use of this language. First, it ignores the Jewish identity of many Holocaust victims. Referring to the Holocaust triggers specific memories, trauma, and reactions in Jews; and when the victims' Jewish identity is ignored, these memories, reactions, and trauma also are ignored. This slight also encourages the culture at large to think of the Holocaust as a kind of evil disconnected from the plight of Jews, desensitizing them to the trauma Jewish people experienced and are still processing. Thus we have analyses of Middle East conflicts without reference to the trauma of the Holocaust; we have people who think Jews are greedy without awareness that Jews were historically routed into banking professions because of religious proscriptions against Christians lending money to other Christians.

Neglecting the identity of Holocaust victims creates a culture of forgetfulness about Jewish injury and trauma. As a therapist, I have learned that many Jews internalize this insensitivity by ignoring or disavowing the connection between their personal suffering and their Jewish identity. As a result, Jews can suffer from various symptoms, both psychological and physical, which they believe are manifestations of their personal problems or pathologies, without considering that these symptoms may be a result of unprocessed trauma related to the Holocaust or anti-Semitism.[7]

In fact, most Jews make no connection between their particular suffering and their Jewish identity. In short, *they ignore their specific history and instead quarantine themselves off into a kind of inner ghetto, thinking something is wrong with them, a form of Jewish shame.*[8]

Second, neglecting the Jewish identity of Holocaust victims dismisses the anti-Semitic roots of the Holocaust. The Holocaust was not only a terrible genocide; it was also a monstrous act of hatred against Jews. Referring to the Holocaust, Nazis, or Hitler, divorced from any analysis or discussion of hatred against Jews, promotes blindness to anti-Semitism today and discourages critical thinking about it among Jews and non-Jews alike. Desensitizing people to anti-Semitism makes it less likely that people will recognize its current practice in the form of humor, preferences for non-Jewish styles of communication, stereotypes about Jewish behavior, or biases about physical attributes (e.g., skin color, nose shape, or hair texture).

When Jews speak up to challenge the offense, they must identify themselves as Jews and risk being subjected to stereotypes about Jewish paranoia and pushiness. However, when anti-Semitism goes unnoticed and unchallenged, Jews are more likely to feel self-critical, fearful, depressed, or disempowered. They may never realize that these symptoms result from being injured by other people's prejudice.[9] Again, an inner ghetto is created, this time to contain reactions to prejudice. And again, Jews are likely to think something is wrong with their reaction—another form of Jewish shame.

Third, neglecting the identity of Holocaust victims minimizes the magnitude of the injury perpetrated by the Nazi regime. A person with a paper cut ought not be equated to a person maimed in a traffic accident; a person slapped in the face ought not be equated to a person beaten with a belt or whip. Comparing the Holocaust to actions or events that either injure no one, or cause injuries that are hardly comparable, minimizes the injury Jews suffered in the Holocaust.

When this kind of comparison regularly occurs without censure, Jews internalize this perspective and learn to minimize their own injury and the magnitude of the efforts required to heal that injury. This minimization causes many Jews to believe that the strength of their feelings, opinions, and reactions to insult are disproportionate and inappropriate. As explored in the essay "I'm

Not a Hypochondriac—I'm Just a Jew," one stereotype suggests that Jews have a tendency toward hypochondria, as if they are pathologically over-concerned with their suffering. Again, Jews end up believing something is wrong with them and ghettoizing the magnitude of their feelings—again, a form of Jewish shame.

The trauma caused by the Holocaust still resonates in the Jewish psyche, causing physical and emotional symptoms that can affect relationships and families.[10] To casually evoke the Holocaust —without bearing witness to the Jewish victims of the injury and the anti-Semitic ideology of its perpetrators—renders the historical trauma invisible, cloaking much Jewish suffering in a veil of shame. The same dynamics exist for other groups who were systematically murdered by the Nazi regime, including Roma, disabled, and LGBTQ people.

Further, all traumatic injuries, including those of abused children, soldiers, and rape victims, evoke the dynamics of dismissal, denial, and shame. All of us must bear witness to these traumatic events, call for greater understanding, and care for the victims. When we do not, we fail to recognize and account for not only the 42,500 Nazi camps and ghettos from more than half a century ago, but also our metaphorical inner camps and ghettos, built out of the denial and ignorance of the trauma that still resonates with many today.

8

I'm Not a Hypochondriac—I'm Just a Jew

Some people, including therapists and humorists, think that being Jewish and being a hypochondriac go hand in hand. They think of Jews and conjure up a neurotic, therapy-going, compulsively worrying Woody Allen type. In fact, Allen himself writes in a recent *New York Times* opinion piece, "Hypochondria: An Inside Look," "I am always certain I've come down with something life threatening. ... Every minor ache or pain sends me to a doctor's office."[1]

While I enjoy a good joke, even at the expense of Jews (and I have happily watched and re-watched many Woody Allen movies), there is a troublesome side to this stereotype.

First, for the purposes of full disclosure, let me say that I am a Jewish therapist (not that there's anything wrong with that). Second, Allen never directly connects Jews and hypochondria, but he doesn't need to because we all get it. We know he's Jewish even though he says he's not religious, a statement often made by Jews who do not want to identify with being Jewish—not just religiously, but culturally as well. (I hear my grandmother saying in her Russian Jewish accent, "Why not say he's Jewish?") Moreover, the title of his essay alone may make readers, Jew and Gentile alike, imagine they are getting let in on a peculiarly Jewish "illness."

Piqued by Allen's article specifically, and the stereotype in general, I called a Jewish colleague of mine, Dr. Gary Reiss, who is an expert on Jewish psychology. He noted that some Jews have a penchant for worrying about, or expressing greater concern over, their physical symptoms. However, he has found that when he takes the symptom and worry seriously, and particularly when he helps the client see themselves as connected to their Jewish history, they feel better. In these cases, the worry was itself a symptom of not having had the fears and psychic trauma relating to Jewish history fully acknowledged. Further, he learned that validating those worries was part of the process of healing from this historical trauma.

I have witnessed the same phenomenon in my own work with Jews. Treating Jewish clients as if their worries were valid and connected to their Jewish history, instead of a figment of their imagination, has had a curative effect.

Speaking more broadly, most symptoms that go unaddressed naturally amplify, whether they are physical, psychological, or social. In essence, our symptoms grow more disturbing until their power cuts through the walls of denial and reaches our awareness, making their meaning known and finally inciting us to action. While some mainstream psychologists (as well as bloggers and comedians) may consider the amplification of fears and worries in the Jewish psyche to be a form of hypochondria, this kind of thinking treats the individual as if their pain and concern were illegitimate and a function of their faulty psychology. The label and diagnosis may thus add insult to injury by dismissing the deeper issue. It can be far more useful, compassionate, and instructive to understand Jewish "hypochondria" as a symptom of the relatively unseen, unexplored, and denied trauma that emanates like a wave across generations.

It's not only Jews who fall prey to this psychological twist. A member of any marginalized group may express aspects of their trauma in confusing ways, only to be viewed by others as if they have an internal problem or sickness.

Being sensitive to humor is a tricky business. There is always a way out for the humorist—"It was just a joke." However, *associating Jews with hypochondria risks pathologizing Jews for taking their pain, trauma, and fears seriously.* At the risk of pushing my argument too strongly, the association just might fail, again, to bear witness to a Jewish trauma. It even risks being, psychologically, a form of Holocaust denial.

Okay, perhaps I am making too much of this; perhaps I have gone too far. Perhaps comparing a relatively innocent, even benign, stereotype to Holocaust denial is just too much.

Or is it that I'm just a Jew who worries too much?

9

Skull and Crossbones:
Projecting onto Folks with HIV/AIDS

"**D**o you know what it's like to have AIDS?" my friend asked. "Everyone looks at you as if you had a skull and crossbones over your head. They treat you like you're already dead."

Another man with AIDS I knew, after waking from a coma, said he believed he had dropped into the coma because he didn't have the strength to fight the constant projections of others. "It's hard to keep living when people insist on seeing me as dead or dying," he said. "I'm not dead yet. I wish people would stop burying me."

As a culture, we are in denial about death. We get sick but resist our own sense of frailty; we witness another's death but deny their mortality; we age but fight against every visible reminder. We are compelled to project death and dying onto other people, and those with HIV/AIDS become prime targets.

Whether people are caring, dismissive, or contemptuous of those with HIV/AIDS, they escape the disquieting experience of seeing their own death in the mirror. But they also forfeit the gifts that awareness of death can bring, the way it can reorganize priorities and bring people closer to their loved ones and spirit.

For people with AIDS, being viewed as diseased or dying saps their energy, devalues the life they are living, and hypnotizes them to stop living before their time. However, because this projection is so pervasive, it is hard for many to fight back, to defend their humanity, to remember that their lives are still full of experiences —feelings, conversations, touch, and spiritual states—not to mention loving and being loved.

This projection doesn't only injure those with HIV. It costs everyone. When sickness and weakness are projected onto another, compassion curdles into pity. People who don't have HIV remain blind to how they can learn from the psychology of HIV.

As a dream analyst, I sometimes imagine an entire community of people coming to my therapy practice with the following dream: There are two groups of people in the community. People in the first group have a weakened immunity and are open to feeling, but defenseless against even the mildest breeze. People in the second group are less sensitive and try to stay away from people in the first group, not wanting to catch their illness.

When the dreamers ask for my interpretation, I say, "The first group needs more protection and care for their vulnerability. The second group needs more contact with life and receptivity to its pains and pleasures. In this way, the whole community can become more healed."

Essentially, those of us who are HIV-negative must learn from those of us who are HIV-positive. We must learn how to lower our guard. Simply put, if we believe that being invulnerable is the key to living a long life, we need to learn that being vulnerable, moved, and affected is what it means to be alive.

I still feel close to my friend who died some fifteen years ago. I can hear him speaking to those who project death and sickness onto those with HIV and AIDS: "We are not dead. We are dying, but so are you. If you were more open to your own frailty, if you were less consumed with overcoming your own insecurity, if your psychological immune system weren't so convinced that it's not you who's dying, it would give many of us a bit of reprieve. And it would give you the chance to touch life more intimately and to know more deeply the beauty of giving and receiving love."

Paging Dr. Ben Carson: Homophobia Calling

A man who is unconscious of himself acts in a blind, instinctive way
and is in addition fooled by all the illusions that arise when he sees
everything that he is not conscious of in himself coming
to meet him from outside as projections upon his neighbour.
—Carl Jung, "The Philosophical Tree"[1]

Certain biases sneak past intelligent minds without the benefit of data, critical thinking, or experience. How can this be?

Consider the case of neurosurgeon and presidential candidate Ben Carson, who had a ready-made theory about homosexuality, plus evidence to prove it. The theory: Being gay is a choice. His evidence: "Because a lot of people who go into prison go into prison straight—and when they come out, they're gay."[2] Later, Carson apologized, saying that he did not know how all gay people become gay.

Why didn't his scientific, rational mind critique his words before they came out of his mouth? Why do people become collaborators in believing and spreading ignorance—especially hurtful ignorance?

Consider the case of Ed, a straight man, a religious man, who believes that these qualities are part of what makes him worthy and good. But Ed has occasional sexual fantasies about men, which he suppresses because he considers them immoral. Rather than engage in critical psychological reflection, Ed judges and disavows these fantasies, finding them inconsistent with the religious beliefs his sense of self relies on. His homosexual impulses are then relegated to Ed's shadow—an unconscious region of his psyche.

Consistent with all shadow aspects of people, Ed projects his own "immorality" onto an "other"; in this case, our gay sisters and brothers. The result: When Ed thinks about issues facing gay people, true reflection is rendered nearly impossible because he is not considering the *real* lives of *real* gay people. Instead, he is considering something called "gay" as manufactured by his psyche—aspects of Ed's nature that he finds onerous.

The door that closes off the shadow from discordant information and critical thinking also closes off the heart from feeling empathy about the harm done to those projected upon.

The simple truth—that being gay is one expression of nature's beauty, truth, and love—is out of reach to Ed's conscious mind, as it was to Ben Carson's mind.

ILLUMINATING THE SHADOW:
BRINGING LIGHT TO CARSON'S BIASES

It is a psychological rule that the brighter the light, the blacker the shadow; in other words, the more rationalistic we are in our conscious minds, the more alive becomes the spectral world of the unconscious.
—Carl Jung[3]

Carson's statement perpetuated two common assumptions. Let's take them one at a time in order to shine the light of honest reflection onto a shadow that is found not only in Carson's psyche, but in the culture at large.

Assumption 1: Being gay is a sickness caused by rape or abuse.
The message here is this: Our LGBTQ sisters and brothers are not acting out of love or nature—in fact, they are not even acting from their right minds. They are sick; being gay is an illness.

Carson is clearly not alone in this viewpoint. The Center for Marriage and Family Studies of the Family Research Council states that "[M]en who sexually molest boys all too often lead their victims into homosexuality and pedophilia."[4]

For much of the 20th century, the American Psychiatric Association also held the view that homosexuality was a mental illness. However, in 1973, they corrected their error, eliminating this diagnostic category. Being gay was no longer considered an illness.[5]

The truth is that being raped in prison does not make a person become gay. The reality is quite the opposite: A gay person entering prison is more likely to be raped.[6]

The research is alarming. Sixty-seven percent of gay and transgender men have been sexually assaulted by another inmate, a rate 15 times higher than in the general inmate population.[7]

The projecting psyche twists the facts so egregiously! Instead of seeing our LGBTQ sisters and brothers as more vulnerable to being abused, it views homosexuality as a sickness that results from being abused.

Indeed, there is a sickness—this kind of thinking!

Assumption 2: Homosexuals are inherently criminal; they are rapists.

Carson's statement suggests that mainstream America should fear "them," should be protected from "them," should not trust "them," and should not befriend "them." "They" are dangerous. This kind of thinking is the hallmark of projection—the creation of an "us and them" —that not only makes distinctions, but colors "them" in a cloak of something so negative that we feel justified in treating "them" inhumanely.

Research shows Carson's logic to be completely opposite from the truth. Gay folks are not likely to end up in prison because they are inherently criminal. Instead, they are more likely to go to prison because they are treated as criminals by their families and the justice system.

Many gay youth are rejected by their families. Twenty-six percent leave their homes and turn to the streets to escape emotional and physical abuse.[8] "Prosecutors frequently file charges against these youth for being 'incorrigible' or beyond the control of their parents or guardians, based largely on the parent's objections to their sexual orientation."[9]

Abuse by families, communities, and an ignorant criminal justice system leads our gay sisters and brothers into jail, *not their sexual identity*. Again, the twisted logic of the projecting psyche views a more vulnerable population as the perpetrating population.

This pattern—of blaming victims as a way of hiding the abuse done by perpetrators—is quite common. Members of marginalized groups are regularly stereotyped as being sick and predatory. For example, Jews were said to murder Christian babies in ritual sacrifices, and black men in the United States were often lynched after being falsely accused of raping white women.

More recently, the Catholic Church tried to lay blame for the sexual abuse of minors at the feet of homosexuality—it was gay clergymen that were at fault, not the Church. In fact, in 2002, the Vatican responded to allegations of sexual abuse by declaring that some gay men should not be ordained as priests.[10]

Once again, the research undermines this thesis, indicating that homosexual men are no more likely than heterosexual men to molest children or to be sexually attracted to children or adolescents.[11] As for lesbian mothers, they almost never abuse their children![12]

THE WORST OF IT: SHAME

I think shame is deadly. And I think we are swimming in it deep.
—Brene Brown[13]

Carson's thinking is not just wrong-headed; it's dangerous. Being looked upon as ill, as a threat, destroys the soul of a person. It teaches them not to trust their own thinking, their own feelings and desires, their own spiritual and moral rightness.

Simply put, it injects a lethal dose of shame into the psyche. The suicide rate of gay teens alone attests to the deadliness of this shaming: gay, bisexual, and questioning youth are three to four times more likely to attempt suicide.[14]

It's time to inject a life-saving dose of critical thinking into our political and social discourse. And it's time for all of us to recognize the moral problem inherent in belief systems that identify their own light as so bright and true that it can only leave an equally dark shadow in its wake.

Hunger, Self-Hatred, Failure, and Sexism: The Real Weight-Loss Story

1

Does America *Really* Need to Go on a Diet?

Fat jokes are fair game, whether told by wannabe comedians in barbershops or professional ones on *The Tonight Show*. When a large person buys an order of French fries, other customers don't hold back their disapproving looks. Reality TV shows, reinforced by jury-type audiences, suggest "tough love" tactics to make family members diet. Programs that promise you can "Lose 8 pounds in 2 weeks" or "Lose 10 pounds in 3 weeks" are a dime a dozen, while actually costing American consumers billions of dollars.

The "Americans need to diet" message comes to us via radio waves, our television sets, the Internet, and the mouths of people around us all the time. Just the other day I read an article on ABC News that warned about the "crisis" of childhood obesity.[1] While I realize that 18% of children ages 6–11[2] and 36% of adults are obese,[3] this message is not the whole truth. In fact, this message blocks out the rest of the weight-loss story.

Consider the following facts: Approximately 30% of girls are overweight or obese.[4] However, 81% of 10-year-olds are afraid of being fat.[5] In addition, more and more research on the relationship between weight and health shows that being overweight, and even mildly obese, does not actually lead to greater health risks,[6] whereas losing weight and gaining it back—perhaps the most common result of diet programs—is clearly linked to health risks.[7]

The barrage of the "Americans need to diet" message is bad medicine for girls and women who have already internalized the fear of being considered fat. Research shows that 97% of women are "cruel to their bodies" every day,[8] while girls ages 11–17 are more afraid of becoming fat than they are of nuclear war, cancer, or losing their parents.[9] It is not only the level of obesity that is alarming; it is the voice in the minds of girls and women that repeats, "I'm fat and ugly," "Nobody will ever want to be with me," and "I'm lazy and disgusting." Further, the "diet" message rarely confronts the powerful objectification of women and women's bodies perpetuated by our mainstream culture.

Related to this is another fact: Not everyone overeats; not everyone is too fat. About 8 million Americans (mostly women) have an eating disorder, and about half of all Americans personally know someone with an eating disorder.[10] And although the health risks related to obesity are real, the health risks of having an eating disorder are arguably worse. The mortality rate associated with anorexia nervosa is 12 times higher than the death rate for *all* causes of death for females 15–24 years old.[11] While an estimated 300,000 deaths per year are due to the obesity epidemic,[12] an estimated 480,000 die of eating disorders.[13] Clearly, many people do need to lose weight and be more mindful of their diet and health; however, at least as many people need to stop worrying about their weight and living in a house built on shame and self-hatred.

To go further still, the "Americans need to diet" message puts all the blame for the problem on individuals and parents. However, the data is quite clear: Diet programs don't work! The $60 billion diet industry[14] has a success rate of 5–10% at best.[15] That means more than 90% of people either don't lose weight or gain it back. It is time to stop perpetuating the myth that if people work hard and follow their diet regimen, they will lose weight. It's simply not true.

Why don't diets work? One reason I have uncovered in my research and work with clients is that people naturally resist criticism and shame. Telling people they are fat and need to lose weight, or telling ourselves we are fat and should diet, is often experienced as criticism leading to shame—something people naturally resist and fight against. It's as if one voice is saying, "You need to lose weight" while another is saying, "I'll never follow your rules and programs." The result: Without some deeper psychological and critical thinking, efforts at dieting will make people *more* ashamed of themselves because they will fail over and over. Simply saying, "Americans need to diet" is likely to have this same shaming effect. In short, this message is more harmful than helpful.

Many Americans need to lose weight; it's true. But haven't we become a little obsessed with dieting and our girth? Isn't it time for more heart to enter the conversation? To those who are stuck on this message, I say, "Please, a little more critical thinking, a little less criticism, and a whole lot more love."

2

Do You Know Why You Eat?
The Key to Losing Weight

Few people are aware of the meaning or purpose behind their eating patterns and tendencies. Most just parrot back what they have been taught about addictions and compulsions, such as, "I medicate my feelings," "It's an unhealthy way that I've learned to care for myself," "It comforts me," or, perhaps most commonly, "I'm screwed up; something is wrong with me."

Discovering the deeper meaning of our eating patterns requires something that most people, including many counselors, do not have: the patience and love of a naturalist who temporarily suspends moral judgment and assumptions about health in order to observe empirical details. This patience and love allows one to carefully and respectfully gather critical, but often ignored, information about the personal and cultural history of the user, the rituals they engage in surrounding food, the qualities of the food they desire, and the feelings or state of mind they experience when eating. After years of study and working with individuals, I have come to believe that without this information, our labors to lose weight, or help others do so, will be in vain.

Consider Jeff, a student who attended my university class called "Addictions and Dependencies." He told the class, quite vulnerably, how upset he was about being overweight and how much he ate. In exploring the history of his eating and weight gain, Jeff recalled that he and his twin sister, at about eight years of age, went to visit their grandmother for a summer visit. They both gained a lot of weight that summer; Jeff never lost his. That was 30 years prior to our conversation. While some may dismiss this detail as irrelevant, uncovering a background story is like finding gold because it can bring understanding and self-love to the healing equation, invaluable resources in making any personal change.

Another important detail is the food a person most desires. I asked Jeff, "What did you eat there?"

"Bread." In fact, he still had a particular affinity for bread.

"When do you eat it?"

"Whenever I feel unhappy or am faced with tasks, like doing homework, that I don't like." He especially loved eating bread at night when he felt alone and wanted something comforting before bed.

I asked Jeff about his preparation rituals. I learned he would make toast (sourdough and cinnamon were his favorites), and when the bread was finely and evenly browned, he buttered it immediately so it would melt just right. One could say he was a toast connoisseur. As he spoke about this ritual, he smacked his lips, his eyes sparkled, and his wonderful smile lit up the room. Jeff's "hunger" came alive. Bringing hunger to the surface is critical if you want to empathize with the person's experience and understand what is deeply motivating them to eat.

Next, we want to help the person "dream"—that is, use their imagination to make closer contact with the part of them that eats. I asked Jeff, "What kind of person are you who loves this bread? Do you have an image or a memory of a person who is like this?"

Jeff said he had an internal image of Wimpy, the Popeye cartoon character who sits at the lunch counter, saying, "I'll gladly pay you Tuesday for a hamburger today."

"What's life like for Wimpy?" I asked.

"Wimpy is sad," Jeff said as his smile faded. "He can never get enough." We had now entered the realm of dreaming and imagination. Tracking a person in this way can open the door to unexplored feelings, needs, and states of mind they may be searching for and expressing in their eating habits.

Many people, including Jeff, would see the "Wimpy" part of himself as something to get over—a greedy, financially irresponsible, depressed soul who overeats. But actually, Jeff didn't have enough of what he really wanted and needed. Wimpy is trying to get what he wants, but his wants and needs are expressed by reaching for bread. If we are going to help him eat less bread, then we need to respect that Wimpy doesn't have enough of something. I wanted to help Jeff figure out what that was and what stops him from reaching for it.

At this point in the investigation, it is critical to explore the beliefs and self-critical voices that stop a person from reaching for what they really want. If we don't make these censors more conscious and help the person stand up against them, they will likely find substances and behaviors that meet their needs and desires in unhealthy ways. This creates a cycle of hunger, reaching out, dissatisfaction, and more hunger—the essence of an addictive pattern.

Jeff believed he should be satisfied with what he had. He said that a "glass half-full" mentality is best; otherwise, it's hard to be happy. This belief led him to try to accept what he had in life even though it was insufficient. However, this same belief acted like a censor, as if it were saying, "Be happy with what you have; your needs and desires are what make you unhappy, not your lack of fulfillment." As a result, in most areas of his life—including his work, relationships, and free time—Jeff tried to be satisfied with what he had. This belief masqueraded as a spiritual belief, which served to disavow his hunger for pleasure and real happiness. He thought that this attitude was mature and reasonable, and that eventually it would lead him to a deeper and more "evolved" happiness. He had not considered the fact that his appetite was voracious.

His belief that he should be happy with what he had served to deny his sadness and his hunger.

The truth was that like Wimpy, Jeff wasn't getting enough. What did he really want? A life as delicious as a perfect piece of toast.

The rest of our conversation was an exploration of what it would be like to feed his deeper hunger, eating as much as he wanted, with a palate geared toward maximum pleasure, not only in his bread eating, but in his life. He said happily that he was considering living life as if he had an insatiable hunger. "For what?" I asked. "For life and all the things I want it to be," he responded.

Jeff is now applying what he learned in his thirty-year course in bread eating to his job, his relationships, and even in class, where he is asking a lot more questions and grabbing considerably more of my attention on breaks and after class. To my satisfaction (mostly), he is asking more and more of me each evening!

This man taught me yet again that some things bear fruit slowly and ripen hidden from our intentions, our goals, and methods. While thirty years of eating bread seems like a long time, and is certainly an unhealthy practice, it is not without reason. Perhaps it is not even that long.

3

Why Diets Fail:
Seven Things You Should Know

The research is clear: diet programs don't work! Professor Steven Hawks of Brigham Young University says, "You would be hard-pressed to review the dietary literature and conclude that you can give people a set of dietary guidelines or restrictions that they will be able to follow in the long term and manage their weight successfully."[1] Dr. Glenn A. Gaesser, in his groundbreaking book *Big Fat Lies: The Truth About Your Weight and Your Health,* concluded that 90% of dieters regain all the weight they lose.[2]

Similarly, professor Traci Mann of UCLA, after conducting a comprehensive analysis of 31 diet studies, concluded that most dieters would have been better off never dieting at all since the majority of them gained all their weight back and more.[3]

From my research and work with clients, I have uncovered seven essential insights about why losing weight is so difficult and what people can do *instead of dieting.*

People who diet often suffer from intense inner and outer criticism.

Most people diet in order to feel better about themselves. This raises the question: What causes overweight people to feel bad about themselves? While you may assume they don't like looking over-weight, a more accurate answer is that along with being overweight comes enormous self-criticism. However, dieting for the purpose of reducing self-criticism often fails because the root of the criticism is often deeper than, and independent of, a person's body size or eating habits. So even though dieters may enjoy temporary relief from self-criticism when they begin to lose weight, this rarely lasts. The self-criticism is rarely extinguished for more than a brief peri-od, and the fundamental critical attitude almost always resurfaces in different ways and with a new focus.

For example, many women disavow their power in the world and in relationships; in essence, they have learned to be fearful of or even antagonistic toward expressing the full measure of their capacities. A woman who has renounced her power often ends up criticizing herself for getting hurt too easily or expressing herself too strongly; and she also tends to be more critical of her body. The power she doesn't use in her outer life turns against her on the in-side! As a result, her inner criticism will not vanish when she tries to lose weight; it will only fade out once she begins to use its power as it should be used—in her relationships and in service of her deepest ambitions.

What to do instead of dieting?

Make a careful accounting of all the things you criticize yourself about each day. How long have you had this critical attitude? Where did it come from? Think of the first time you were ever criticized. Imagine that you really didn't deserve that criticism. How would you have liked to be treated instead? What would you say to that person if you could?

Because people naturally resist shame and self-hatred, they subconsciously undermine diets motivated by these feelings.

Inner criticism about our bodies is invariably mean-spirited, ignorant, and devoid of spiritual value. Thus, it is often far healthier to reject such criticism than to accept it and act on it. In fact, taking a stand against this criticism is an act of power and self-love that not only helps relieve the inner criticism but can also make losing weight easier.

It is self-love that leads people to resist following through with the diet programs they put themselves on. However, this concept is so counterintuitive that most dieters will say, "I diet because I care about myself, and I fail to follow through because of my inadequacy."

I worked with a woman recently who had suffered long and hard to lose weight. Some months she did better than others; some years she did better than others. One day she said to me, "I just want to like myself regardless of my weight." Those were some of the sweetest words I ever heard her speak. "What do you like about yourself?" I asked. We sat in silence awhile. I am sure some part of her had been waiting far longer than those minutes we sat together. After a bit, I decided to help her by beginning, "I like the purity of your words and desire; I like your simplicity. I like your humanity. I like your spirit. I like how I feel being with you when you talk like this." We both smiled, teary-eyed.

What to do instead of dieting?

Stop criticizing and shaming yourself for not sticking to your diet plan. Have it out with your critic! Make your critic's words explicit—say them clearly, out loud, and then fight back as intelligently and fiercely as you can. This exercise will support your self-love by building a more empowered self. Going further, make a list of other plans, activities, and people you would like to say "no" to and begin practicing immediately.

For example, my client Sandra tried to lose weight for years, failing over and over. She was embarrassed to go out, wear certain clothes, order certain foods, or approach men to whom she felt attracted. I modeled the inner criticism she expressed to me by saying, "You're fat. You should stay at home. You ought to be ashamed of yourself. And certainly, you shouldn't think you are worthy of having a partner you are attracted to!" At first she looked wounded and deflated, but when I encouraged her to fight back, she began to stand up straighter and smile. Just thinking about resisting her inner criticism made her feel better. I asked Sandra in which other areas of her life she was going along with a program or person when she really didn't want to. She said it happened at work and sometimes with her children. Her homework was to say "no" to these people more often.

When a person is "bigger" and more powerful than they realize, they unconsciously resist programs designed to make them "smaller."

Many people, especially women, live inside a box that is too small for their intelligence, creativity, feelings, and spirit. However, their bodies often find a way of manifesting the "bigness" that they suppress. The result: When they diet to make their bodies smaller, their psyches experience this as an attempt to shrink their strength and therefore find ways to resist and derail their efforts. In the words of the big blue Genie in Disney's *Aladdin*, "Phenomenal cosmic power! Itty bitty living space!"

Consider Sally, who had been called "stocky," "hefty," and a "big girl" since she was young. She spent much of her life trying to lose weight so that she could shed those descriptions and look more like her sister and other girls. She experienced further criticism during her military service, when she was told that her thighs were too big, even though she could meet all the benchmarks for strength, agility, and speed. She even spread Preparation H on her thighs at night and wrapped them in Saran Wrap to shrink them! Years later, she wanted to become an emergency medical technician and asked if I thought she should not push herself so hard. She was a big woman with big power and big ambitions, but she was still trying to make herself smaller. She soon achieved her career goal and was happy doing so.

What to do instead of dieting?

Get to know the ways you are more powerful, beautiful, intelligent, and incredible than people (especially you) think you are. Name your qualities and identify the boxes you live in that are too small. Share your insights with a good friend.

It takes power and courage to give up a diet program that is not right for you.

People use massive amounts of resources—financial, emotional, intellectual, and psychological—to lose weight. But they rarely ask themselves a key question: "What part of me doesn't go along with this agenda?" That part, the one that resists, stands up against a massive assault of criticism and prevails—*by not sticking with the program!* The problem is, most people have no relationship with this part of themselves other than treating it as the enemy. When people integrate that power, they can move mountains. When they fight it, they lose.

What to do instead of dieting?

Instead of thinking of yourself as a failure and feeling accordingly, imagine how much power it would take to stand up against the negative opinions you and others have about you at your current weight. Imagine what it would take to successfully resist all the efforts you make to lose weight. Now, think of a person you know who has enough power to be unmoved by those efforts and opinions. What do you think it would take for them to stand firm—self-love, courage, power, belief, faith, good friends, or family support? Finally, imagine you are a person who has that kind of power. In what areas do you most need it? Make a list of who and what else in your life you would resist if you had that power, such as authority figures, rules about how to behave, etc.

Eating preferences and patterns are subtle, yet profound, indications about our beliefs and life paths.

Counselors, diet-program developers, and the rest of us need to get it through our heads that people are not stupid, lazy, ugly, ignorant, undisciplined, or otherwise pathological. We act in certain ways, including our eating patterns and preferences, for reasons that are meaningful and worthy of our deepest compassion and understanding. If eating, dieting, and body image are the issues you wrestle with, then the details of what and how you eat are great tools for *finding the source of your authentic nature*.

I am reminded of a woman who loved rum raisin ice cream. She was a spiritual seeker and diligent meditator. To find out what motivated her to eat the ice cream, I said, "Listen deeply to yourself as you imagine tasting the ice cream." She heard an "Om" sound in her heart that helped her connect with her most profound spiritual experiences. In many ways, her ice cream experience was closer to what she sought than the states she achieved in meditation. She learned that her meditation needed to feel more like rum raisin ice cream and less like the harsh discipline she was accustomed to.

What to do instead of dieting?

Think of one of your favorite foods. Carefully and mindfully become aware of what it feels like to enjoy it. Do not criticize yourself. Simply pay full attention to your experience by noting your feelings (euphoric, relaxed, dreamy, excited), looking for inner images (children, elders, clouds, birds, gorillas), and listening for sounds and tunes. Focus on those feelings, images, and tunes. You may want to dance your feelings, draw the images, and playfully exaggerate aspects of them that attract you, or hum and sing the tunes. Imagine that this is a way of living. How is it different from the way you live? This is what you are truly hungry for!

When people become more attuned to their authentic selves, changing their eating preferences and patterns is easier and more sustainable.

Despite the fact that weight-loss agendas usually focus on food and exercise, the psychological truth is, *there is no substitute for living a fuller and more authentic life in winning the weight loss battle.* What we need is not a weight-loss plan, but a plan for how to live a more fulfilling life. I have spoken to many people who mysteriously lost weight when they changed relationships or careers, started expressing their creativity more, or addressed social biases that hurt them. None of these have anything to do with food or exercise!

What to do instead of dieting?
Ask yourself, "What do I want from life?" What changes would you make in your life if you were entirely free? Would you go back to school, look for a new job, ask your boss for a promotion, plant a garden, paint a room a new color, pray more, or even stop and do nothing? Take stock of the fantasies that arise, and seriously consider how you might begin to integrate even a few of these changes into your life.

When people change the way they perceive their bodies, their relationships often change as well.

Our bodies are intelligent. While we spend much of our time try-ing to get our bodies to conform to our desires, we actually need to spend more time having our desires conform to the wisdom of our bodies. Listening to our body's wisdom requires us to develop a true respect for the intelligence contained in our body's desires (in terms of food) as well as for our body size and shape (e.g., its roundness, softness, or largeness). For example, many of my clients have found a sense of protection in the size of their bodies, a pro-tection they needed in their relationships. Others have found that what they hungered for in the foods they ate were qualities that were missing in their relationships with their partners. In other words, building a loving relationship with their bodies led to breaking out of forms of relationship that no longer fit.

I remember a woman who believed that her husband was an ally in her weight-loss efforts. He reminded her of her goals and praised her successes. However, upon developing a more loving re-lationship with her body, she began to see that he was also critical of the way she looked. He supported her weight loss not only be-cause he cared for her but also because he didn't like the way she looked. She had grown so accustomed to not liking her body that she repressed the offense she felt when he tacitly agreed with her dislike. Further, she noticed her husband was not only critical of her body but of other aspects of her as well.

What to do instead of dieting?
Consider the possibility that you feel put down, disrespected, misun-derstood, and not heard in one or more of your relationships. For a moment, fully trust your feelings; don't analyze them or try to de-termine if they are right or appropriate. Now imagine you are your own best friend, someone who would fully advocate for your feel-ings. What would this friend say to the person who disrespects you?

4

Trying to Lose Weight?
Satisfy Your *Real* Hungers

"**S**top eating bread, pizza, donuts, snacks, sugar, hamburgers, ice cream. Just do it." Sounds simple. While this advice may help temporarily, the research is clear: it rarely makes a difference in the long term. This kind of counsel focuses on individuals' inadequacies (lack of discipline, control, intention, and purpose). It rarely offers ways to deepen personal transformation, and it shames us in the process.

What can you do? Respect your hunger! The hunger for your favorite foods is wired to your hunger for life. Consider the following cases.

Make Me One with Everything

A woman tries to lose weight but loves hamburgers. She tries to eat them without the bun, without the cheese, without the ketchup and mayonnaise mixture she loves. But this just makes her hungry for a "real" hamburger later.

I say, "Tell me how good those hamburgers are. Make me want one."

She describes a fabulous hamburger with everything; her description makes my mouth water.

"Must you have everything on it?" I ask. "Can't you give up something?"

"I always give up something," she says. "I never get exactly what I want in life."

She wanted a "hamburger life," with everything. And until she created more of that, the power of an actual hamburger was too hard to fight. I helped her create a diet program that started with her compromising less about what she wanted in life. She not only lost weight, but she also changed her relationships and went back to school—a life dream.

And on the Seventh Day, Häagen-Dazs

A man tries to lose weight but loves Häagen-Dazs chocolate chip ice cream. He resists walking down the frozen-food aisle in the grocery store but goes out later to buy an ice cream cone down the street. Sometimes there is no ice cream in the house, and he feels down that evening and wakes up sad the next day.

I say, "Tell me about eating chocolate chip ice cream."

"It's the end of the day. My chores and work are over, and I just want to sit back and relax before bed. That's when it hits."

"Imagine your day is done and you have a spoonful in your hand. Taste it."

"Mmm, it's good. The whole day feels good somehow."

"The whole day feels good?"

"Yes. Even God rested after the sixth day and looked upon his work and blessed it."

This man wanted more than simple comfort; he wanted a time to reflect, acknowledge, and affirm his day. The ice cream was more than just a sweet reward; he was hungry for feeling good about what he had accomplished. As he made time with his spouse to review the day's successes, not only did the hunger for ice cream diminish, but also a truer, deeper appreciation for his work and his contribution to the family grew.

Hungry for Starbucks; Hungry for Happiness

Erin is 28 years old. Big-boned and strong, she is forthright and candid; her eyes look unwaveringly at me. Erin tells me she has dealt with weight issues for a year and a half.

"What's your favorite food?" I ask.

"Starbucks caramel mochas, 16-ounce. I used to order them with whole milk. Now I use 2%, but they're not as good. They make me less fat, but the old ones were better. Sometimes I drink two in a day when things are really bad." *Erin describes them with bright eyes. It's as if she is talking about a great discovery, like a miner reaching a vein of gold.*

I say, "Let go of all the criticism you have about your weight and drinking these mochas. Tell me what it's like to drink one." *It's key that a person not speak from judgment about their eating.*

"They are just delicious. I look forward to them. I leave my house to get one, and I live 20 minutes away from the nearest Starbucks." *She laughs with a kind of pride at her determination and continues,* "It's stupid to place so much importance on a cup of coffee." *I notice that she is holding onto a plastic cup that was once filled with water.*

"I am noticing your hands wrapped around that cup," I say. "Can you show me what your hands are doing? Take them off the cup and show me how they are holding the cup."

"They are like claws." *She takes her hands off the cup; her fingers express a powerful tension.*

"Grab the water bottle on the table with those clawlike hands of yours." *I want her to express the potency and passion in her "claw," but the cardboard cup would simply crumble, so I offer her the hard plastic bottle in front of us.* "Notice your hand—how it grasps and holds.

Notice the firmness, the intention, the feeling of your grip. When you're ready, I am going to try to pull it away from you. Allow yourself to react freely." *I want Erin to make conscious contact with the part of her that won't let go—a part that is mostly unconscious but that rules the moment by compelling her to do something she is also strongly against. If Erin and I can't bring out the power of her desire, we will never know what we are up against and will likely fail. It would be like fighting an enemy that keeps defeating us and never learning anything about that enemy.*

Erin smiles mischievously, and as we look at each other, she begins to laugh. We both know, instantly, how strong and determined she is. I pull the bottle toward me. Her muscles became taut, her jaw stiffens, and her eyes become even more fixed as she pulls the bottle toward herself, resisting my force.

"What are you doing?" I ask.

"I am holding onto the coffee."

"Let go. Why do you need the coffee so much? Why are you holding onto it so dearly?" *I try to wrestle the cup from her so she can feel her grip, her desire, and her unwillingness to let go. I'm acting like her current diet program, which treats her caramel mochas as something to take away instead of understand.*

"It's my happiness." *Erin and I are both surprised; neither of us had expected this answer.*

"Happiness? Why do you have to have to fight for your happiness?"

"Because I don't have it." *Her eyes tear up.* "I can get it at Starbucks. I've placed my happiness into this one thing. Because if I need it, I can just go out and get it."

"What stands in the way of your happiness? *We are now on the road to exploring how to get what she really needs in her life. If I can help her get her happiness, it will be easier for her to relinquish her grip on the one thing she knows how to reach for, grasp, and fight for—the caramel mochas.*

"My family, my parents, my work. I want to focus more on myself and my own career. I want to be put first. I want to snap my fingers and have everybody do what I say. But I am always having to fit into a shape defined by other people and responsibilities."

"Can you imagine being that kind of person, who snaps her fingers and gets what she wants?"

"It must be nice. I don't know; I never had that. I think that is being spoiled. Except that I can snap my fingers and drive twenty minutes to Starbucks. I don't know if I can make other life changes that easily."

Erin and I subsequently developed a weight-loss program based on the insight she had. Yes, this included some additional exercise goals and an effort to be more aware of drinking caramel mochas. But the program also helped her clarify the life changes she wanted to make and gave her the emotional support she needed to make those changes.

One year later, Erin was divorced, pursuing new career options, exercising like a bandit, and at the weight she wanted to be. She snapped her fingers and grabbed her happiness. For Erin, her hunger and thirst for Starbucks coffee was actually a hunger for her real life—a life that would make her truly happy.

Initially, these three clients had created diet programs that not only deprived them of the food they wanted, but also of the lives they wanted. Their approach was based on the same thinking that most diet programs rely on. They thought they could somehow overpower, get rid of, or deny their hungers. However, the truth is that people's hungers are powerful and contain profound intelligence. In working with dozens of people who wanted to lose weight, I haven't met a single person whose eating habits were not meaningful. And I haven't met a single person who knew, beforehand, what the meaning was—what they were hungry for—without deeper investigation.

Simply put, people are not lazy, stupid, or undisciplined. Nor are they just suffering from low self-esteem or a lack of care for their bodies and health. The experience of tens of thousands of dieters shows that despite all the negatives that get heaped on people who are heavy or obese—health problems, inner criticism and shame, outer criticism and prejudice—the hungers that drive people to eat are even more powerful.

While many consider this to be bad news (because it is not always easy to uncover inner hungers), there is more than a silver lining. Who we really are—our deepest needs, wants, and desires— will not easily be ignored, silenced, or pushed aside. Even under great adversity, our authentic selves prevail. Even under the gaze of critical eyes, we still assert ourselves, albeit in a less-than-ideal way.

And the news gets better. If we discover what our deeper hungers are and begin to create a life more consistent with those hungers, changing what we eat gets a whole lot easier.

5

Shame, Body Image, and Weight Loss

When a person looks in the mirror or steps on a scale and doesn't like what they see, they often say to themselves, "My arms are flabby." "My belly rolls in on itself." "My thighs are too big." "This shirt looks terrible on me." Studies have found that both men and women tend to view a woman as separate body parts and a man as a whole body, a phenomenon that furthers the objectification of women's bodies.[1] In fact, a study by *Glamour* magazine found that 97% of women are "cruel to their bodies" every day.[2]

These criticisms are an assault. They have the capacity to hurt and injure, but they do not shame. However, the story rarely stops there. Another part of the person, an internalized witness, says, "You are lazy." "Why did you eat that ice cream last night?" "How come you can't stay on a diet?" "You eat too much comfort food." "Can't you deal with your emotional problems and lose more weight?" This internalized witness ignores that there was an assault, demonstrates no compassion for the pain, and blames the person (the victim) for their suffering. Making matters even more egregious, many people, especially girls, perceive themselves to be overweight when they are not! (For example, a study by *Teen* magazine found that 50-70% of normal-weight girls think they are overweight.[3])

A powerful example of this kind of shaming occurred on an

episode of *Dr. Phil,* where Dr. Phil was trying to help women lose weight before their weddings.[4] The entire premise of the episode was shaming. The guests on the show all had criticisms of their bodies (the assault), but instead of defending them from this criticism or responding to the pain they suffered as a result, Dr. Phil colluded with their assessment (and the culture's assessment) that they were too big. His failure to witness the injury of this criticism denied it and shamed them. He proceeded as if these women felt pain because of their body size, not because of the *criticism* of their body size. In this way, he blamed the victim of the assault. To avoid this kind of shaming, he would have had to do something unusual: consider the possibility that these women didn't need to lose weight to feel better about themselves.

Later in the show, Dr. Phil had thinner women parade across the stage wearing the wedding dresses that his guests were hoping to wear, *but in a smaller size.* While Dr. Phil intended to motivate these women to lose weight, he in fact inflicted more pain on these women by comparing them to other women whom society considers to be more attractive. Again, the assault went unnoticed, the pain not witnessed, leaving Dr. Phil's guests to think, "How can I lose more weight? Why can't I look like that?" They walked away thinking they suffered because they couldn't "fix" themselves, not because they were being criticized on national TV for their body size. Further, those guests who don't lose weight, or who lose it and gain it back (probably almost all of them), are likely to think, "What's wrong with me?" Their shame will be amplified.

What would a non-shaming witness do? To help answer this question, we need to consider what is happening psychologically. Imagine women were paraded across a stage in front of dozens of people, two at a time, while someone said to the first woman, "You are pretty, attractive, beautiful," and to the second woman, "You are fat and unattractive. Why can't you look like her?" while pointing to the first woman. This is the kind of inner criticism and comparison that is happening inside these women and in the minds of some audience members. Would you sympathize with the second woman? Would you be able to defend her? If you could speak to that judge, what would you say? How would you challenge or educate them?

If you would sympathize with the second woman and if you could defend her, then you already know how to be a non-shaming witness and you already know how to bring healing to a shaming event. You have the capacity to bring healing to yourself and many others by speaking about your feelings and perceptions.

Further, if you are willing to speak up on behalf of others, the people you defend will be less likely to think there is something wrong with them. And when people don't believe something is wrong with them, they are less likely to go on diets that don't work.

If more people believed in themselves, perhaps 81% of 10-year-olds wouldn't be afraid of being fat.[5] Perhaps people would believe the findings that being overweight (and even mildly obese) doesn't lead to greater health risks,[6] whereas gaining and losing weight does.[7] And perhaps people would be more likely to defend themselves from the criticism of a culture that demeans and objectifies the bodies of girls and women.

6

Resolving to Lose Weight?
Consider This First

Certainly you want to be healthier. Of course you think that losing weight will make you feel better about yourself. How could you not worry about your friend who really needs to go on a diet? And is it really possible to watch TV, search the Internet, or flip through a magazine and not be confronted with advertisements about losing weight? A $60-billion-dollar industry is banking on your pain, shame, and failure to lose weight.[1]

But before you sign on the dotted line, resolve to lose weight, or muster the chutzpah to finally speak to your friend, listen to the words I have heard clients say to themselves about their bodies:

You are fat, disgusting.

Look at those arms, those breasts, those jowls.

Food is evil and will make you fat and ugly.

No one will ever want to be with you.

You don't deserve anything.

You lazy, stupid shit.

Better to stay home, where people can't see you.

You ugly, worthless, fat bitch. What is wrong with you that you can't lose a few pounds?

Imagine you were listening to a person say these words to someone you loved. Would your first impulse be to suggest a new diet program or exercise strategy? Or would you be moved to stop the violence and assess the damage first? Please, dear readers, be kind to yourselves and those around you who suffer from body shame and struggle with their weight. The violence and wounding is deeper and more hurtful than you may think.

7

Think Your Diet Needs More Discipline?
Think Again

If we listen to the words of authors, therapists, dieticians, physicians, nutritionists, and coaches, we will believe that to lose weight, we must be disciplined. Without discipline, these voices say, we won't be able to stick to our weight-loss strategy. We will fail. However, this advice is only half true and can easily betray our best efforts and intentions. There are two reasons for this, and both involve how people apply discipline to their diet strategies.

First, discipline is often used in a punitive manner, leading to a cycle of seeming success and failure. While the word "discipline" has the same root as "disciple," suggesting the loving relationship between a student and mentor, the actual practice of *being disciplined* is often accompanied by an attitude of self-correction and chastisement, especially for those who were raised in a more punishing culture or family environment.

As a result, many of us understandably rebel against being disciplined by not following through on our weight-loss strategy. Essentially, what looks like rebelling and derailing our efforts may actually be a self-loving reaction to a punitive atmosphere that needs to change.

Second, discipline often fails to take into account the deeper motivations for our current eating patterns. We are hungry for something, and that hunger is real and must be fed. While food may not the best way to feed that hunger, simply fighting our hungers or trying to overcome them is a recipe for failure that results in enormous inner criticism. We must identify and address our real hungers.

Further, the reasons people give for their eating patterns seldom turn out to be the deeper reasons that compel them to eat. For example, I can't tell you the number of times people have told me they eat to comfort themselves or to relieve stress. While these reasons appeal to our common sense, they are almost always more superficial and less nuanced than the real underlying needs and are therefore rarely helpful. Uncovering the real needs takes more than an armchair diagnosis or bumper-sticker answer. It requires a clear and loving awareness of the positive feelings we have when we eat, and it means supporting ourselves to reach out for those feelings in our lives.

Plainly stated, dietary discipline without regard for our true underlying hungers is rarely sustainable.

Case Study: Fanny's Story

Fanny, in her mid-fifties, had tried one diet after another for most of her life, without success. When I met her, she said she had finally figured it out. "I was too passive," she explained. "I had become a couch potato. I needed more discipline." We explored the meaning of discipline and whether it was really the answer to her dilemma. Here is an excerpt from our conversation:

Fanny: I finally got it. Time to fight the passivity of watching TV and staying in the house. Time to be disciplined. I now walk twice in the morning and don't sit on the couch so much. *Fanny's voice was fierce, like a drill sergeant.*

David: Show me what you mean. Talk to me as if I were you needing this discipline you speak of.

Fanny: *Fanny grabbed me as if she were going to shake me.* You need to do something about your weight. You can't afford to waste any more years of passivity. You need to take control. You have high blood pressure, high cholesterol—a whole range of problems. You have been on antidepressants. Enough already!

David: *I spoke as Fanny.* Keep grabbing me. Go ahead and shake me up. Shake me out of my passivity. Shake up my whole life. *She grabbed and shook me with impressive force, and I realized that this force wanted to do more than change her exercise and eating habits and that her passivity was about life changes beyond those of weight loss.*

Fanny: Interesting. When you asked me to shake you up, you mentioned life changes. I have found that whenever I have traveled abroad or moved to a different place, I immediately drop forty pounds. It just happens by itself. *Fanny had discovered an important insight: that in the past she has lost weight naturally, without trying to make herself eat differently or exercise more.*

David: *I continued speaking as Fanny so she could talk to herself.* Are you saying that walking two times a day is not the only answer? Are there other ways of addressing my weight issues— other life changes like traveling or living in another culture?

Fanny: You've got to free yourself to do more things. You should break out of prison.

David: How am I in prison?

Fanny: You can be in prison in many ways. Sometimes in your relationship, sometimes in your job—anywhere. In fact, you often find yourself feeling in prison in your job.

David: How can I break out of the prison of my job?

Fanny: Join the Peace Corps. Live in a different culture. You've been thinking about this for a long, long time.

David: You mean I don't only have to go outside my house and walk twice in the morning—I need to change the entire culture I live in, get outside the whole box, the whole prison?

Fanny: Exactly. All those cultural forces that bombard people about who they're supposed to be and how they're supposed to live. When you are outside the culture, you don't have to buy into those.

Fanny went on to say that she had lost large amounts of weight several times in her life—a couple of times when she broke out of bad relationships and other times when she left her job or went overseas. She lost weight when she "broke out of prison." Her passivity wasn't about eating and exercising; it was about her life.

Fanny thought discipline was the answer to her weight problem, but our work together revealed another story. For Fanny, losing weight related more to the life and culture she was living within and less to diet and exercise. So although Fanny was applying greater discipline, she was applying it to a life she didn't want, to a way of living that was not feeding her, making it likely that she would resist these efforts at discipline.

Further, I learned that the culture Fanny was referring to was not only a literal one, requiring a move to a different country. It was also the psychological culture she lived in—her beliefs, attitudes, and values—that she needed to break free from. Working on her own inner culture helped relieve her of her craving for certain foods.

What's Going On?
Reflections on Current Events

1

Philip Seymour Hoffman
and the Shadow of Individual Addiction

After Philip Seymour Hoffman's death on February 2, 2014, the U.S. media obsessively focused for several weeks on his heroin addiction and the growing number of heroin users in this country. If you opened the pages of the *New York Times*, read articles and blogs on *The Huffington Post*, or tuned your channel to any of the cable news shows, you couldn't avoid the opinions of an expert or pundit on this issue. I am not trying to minimize the serious problem of individual substance abuse; the collateral damage to addicts' psyches, bodies, families, and communities is immense. But left in the shadow of the focus on Hoffman, heroin, and other addicts is the fact that we live in a *culture* of addiction.

For example, our culture is addicted to market values. This is not just a figure of speech: We "use" buying, selling, consuming, hustling, saving, stealing, and earning in ways that literally alter our states of mind and how we feel about ourselves, just like the way we use substances. Some folks profoundly depend on these feelings and states, need more and more to maintain their highs, and go through a hellish withdrawal when their patterns are threatened or removed. People with millions of dollars can be afraid to lose a thousand dollars; for many, their feelings about themselves and their lives are totally dependent on whether the stock market goes up or down that day. And while some may say that the collateral damage of heroin or other substances is worse, in the wake of our addiction to market values are destroyed relationships (as a result of painful conflict), children neglected or otherwise harmed, abandoned poor folks who suffer and die, a used and abused Earth and her resources, and a disparaging of so-called "third world" nations—not to mention indigenous people, who often hold non-consumerist values.

We are also addicted to gender stereotypes and harmful myths about what it means to be male and female, which ripple out in a variety of ways, harming girls and boys in the form of sexual assault, fueling deadly eating disorders primarily among girls and women, and propagating homophobic violence. How is this an addiction? Many men, as well as women, depend on gender stereotypes to give them a sense of security and power as well as to protect them from feelings of weakness. If this cloak of power gets disturbed or threatened, men can become depressed or violent, just as people do when they try to abstain from addictive substances. And many women are hooked on shaping their behaviors and bodies into a culturally appealing form, as evidenced by the $60 billion diet industry and the seven million women and one million men with eating disorders. In fact, I have seen as many women addicted to dieting and weight-loss efforts as those addicted to destructive patterns of eating.

I haven't yet met a person who is not struggling with addiction at some level. People are addicted to money, relationship dynamics, salt, sugar, coffee, exercise, even supposedly healthy foods like carrot juice (which can be used and held onto in a way that is powerful and violent). I'm not saying that these substances and behavioral patterns are always addictions. But they become addictions when they are a specific way to access feelings that are otherwise out of reach and when their removal is met with physical or emotional symptoms of withdrawal.

Why do I bring this up? Because I am protesting the idea that addiction is only an individual problem or disease carried by certain people. Because when we don't include this shadow of individual addiction—our culture of addiction—we suffer from a malignant projection onto "those addicts" while we remain unconsciously ignorant, condescending, or full of pity.

2

Diagnosing Depression in the Wake
of Robin Williams's Suicide

The suicide of Robin Williams brought to light the importance of diagnosing depression. Most discussions, articles, and blog posts published in the wake of his death focused on the value of mental-health diagnosis. However, it is also worthwhile to examine the harm that diagnosis may cause. Both of these perspectives are needed; both sides together create a whole picture. In this essay, I discuss the pros and cons of diagnosis.

Pro: Being able to diagnose symptoms
may be the first step in healing; it may even save lives.

From the perspective of mainstream psychology and psychiatry, in order to properly treat patients and relieve their symptoms, we must first categorize symptoms in a way that helps us understand the underlying pathology and that enables clinical research to determine the effectiveness of various treatments.

Several individuals I spoke with highlighted the value of diagnosis. One said, "For me, a formal diagnosis was a godsend, really. It provided an explanation for what was happening to me and opened up opportunities for treatment and medication that are just not available without a psychological diagnosis." Another said, "For me, getting diagnosed with and medicated for depression and anxiety probably saved my life." Clearly, diagnosis does have real value for some people.

Pro: Diagnosis can protect people from ignorant criticism, projection, and shame.

According to Richard Bentall, Ph.D., and Nick Craddock, M.D., a diagnosis "can reduce stigma by explicitly acknowledging the presence of illness (and, thus, that the feelings or behavior cannot be dismissed as character weakness or bloody-mindedness)."[1]

In the words of one woman I spoke with, "It let people know that I was not lazy, stupid, or bizarre." A diagnosis can be akin to saying, "There is nothing wrong with you as a person morally or intellectually. I see you're not simply resisting acting functionally or appropriately."

Pro: Diagnosis can legitimize a person's symptoms, pain, and suffering.

Receiving a diagnosis is often met with an experience of significant relief and helps people develop more understanding of and compassion for themselves. A diagnosis removes the mystery of their symptoms, encourages them to take themselves seriously, and lets them know they are not alone, that others suffer similarly.

"Diagnosis, in a way, legitimized my struggles," said one person. "It was a real thing!" Another said, "Finally, I understood so many of my behaviors that had made me feel misunderstood my whole life." A third person said her brother's diagnosis was freeing "because it identified that there are a lot of other people like him: weird, awesome, and sometimes hurting, too."

Con: Labels stigmatize people, treating them like they are broken and abnormal.

Diagnosis creates labels that can stigmatize individuals, causing them to be viewed as "different from others in ways that are undesirable and shameful."[2] Research shows that stigmas lead to social separation, status loss, and discrimination.[3] Specifically, people

who are labeled "depressed" are often viewed as unstable, unreli-
able, and even dangerous. Further, research by the National Insti-
tutes of Health found that people internalize their diagnostic
labels and begin to see themselves in these same negative ways.[4]

Making matters worse, Jerry Kennard, Ph.D., warns that, "The
label itself becomes self-fulfilling and can bias the way clinicians
and the public see the person. Ordinary aches and pains, grumbles
or personal setbacks, may seen [sic] as symptoms of the disease.
Even the patient can fall into the trap of behaving in ways they
think are expected of them."[5]

Con: Diagnosing individuals dismisses family and societal factors that contribute to the condition.

Most healing paradigms focus on diagnosing, understanding, and
treating an individual who is the "identified patient." While some
individuals do need extra care, this approach can dismiss the role
played by other people, communities, and cultures. For example,
individuals who are more sensitive to abusive situations, toxic at-
mospheres, or hurtful cultural biases are readily viewed as "sick,"
while the families, organizations, or cultures they are reacting to
are likely to be viewed as healthy and to remain untreated.

Salvador Minuchin, founder of Structural Family Therapy, enlightened a generation of therapists when he reported that the
children he treated were symptomatic not because they were sick
but because they were expressing their family's problems. While
those children were the identified patients, the whole family was in
fact ill.[6] Identifying one person as the patient not only marginalizes them, causing them to feel responsible for the family's troubles,
but it also bypasses a more complete understanding of the illness
and how to treat it.

Similarly, some indigenous cultures consider the individual
who expresses a symptom to have a special gift or sensitivity for
expressing a problem that belongs to the tribe. Folks who suffer
mental illness are bearers of information and even healing for their

families as well as for the larger culture and the planet. From this point of view, we can treat those who bear symptoms as teachers, healers, and messengers of the early warning signs about a collective illness requiring treatment in all of us. This could lead us to not only think, "How could we have helped *them*? What were *they* hiding? What was wrong with *them*?" but also ask these questions of ourselves.

African shaman Malidoma Somé, Ph.D., puts it this way: "What those in the West view as mental illness, the Dagara people regard as 'good news from the other world.' The person going through the crisis has been chosen as a medium for a message to the community that needs to be communicated from the spirit realm."[7]

Con: Diagnosis ignores deeper processes that often lead to the discovery of gifts.

When we view a person as if something is wrong with them, we may neglect to see what is "right" and intelligent about their symptoms. For example, Dr. Somé noted that a person who was sent to a mental institution for "nervous depression" was exhibiting the same symptoms he observed in the collective mentality of his village. Writes Stephanie Marohn, "What struck Dr. Somé was that the attention given to such symptoms was based on pathology, on the idea that the condition is something that needs to stop. This was in complete opposition to the way his culture views such a situation. As he looked around the stark ward at the patients, some in straitjackets, some zoned out on medications, others screaming, he observed to himself, 'So this is how the healers who are attempting to be born are treated in this culture. What a loss!'"[8]

Con: Not all depressions are the same; treating them as such can be ineffective at best and harmful at worst.

While the label "depression" creates the sense that depression is a singular condition requiring treatment by anti-depressants, not all depressions are the same. Thus, "anti-depressing" may not be the most effective form of therapy. For example, many people describe depression as a feeling or energy of going down. That person may slump in their chair, their tone of voice may trail off, their head may hang downward or to one side. In such cases, it is sometimes helpful to support the person to "go down" further, to relax, surrender, let go, or even lie down and close their eyes. This helps some people discover deeper feelings they were unaware of (e.g., resentments, a sense of floating and ease, weariness with the life they are living) or values they are pushing aside as they try to cope with a more "normal" life. Treating a person in this situation as if they need lifting up or anti-depressing can miss the meaning behind the depression and the direction they need to pursue for sustainable relief.

In contrast, some people describe depression with anger in their voice. They sound pissed off at themselves and their lack of energy. In some cases, these people are putting themselves down or are being put down by others. They may be more served by accessing their "angry energy" in order to fight against this kind of bullying. Their angry energy is actually an attempt to anti-depress.

Con: While drug treatment for mental illness can be healing and save lives, it can also be ineffective and unsafe for some patients.

Research in the field of psychoactive drugs, including those used to treat depression, is regularly tainted by the financial conflicts of interest of those aligned with the pharmaceutical industry. The Institute of Medicine (US) Committee on Conflict of Interest in Medical Research, Education, and Practice asserts that "Individual and institutional financial interests may unduly influence professional judgments. ... Such conflicts of interest threaten the integrity of scientific investigations, the objectivity of medical education, the quality of patient care, and the public's trust in medicine."[9]

For example, we know that the data on antidepressant medications is skewed because unfavorable results rarely get published.

Research findings are withheld so routinely that while certain drugs are deemed safe and effective, a more thorough review of the research found that the risks outweighed the benefits for almost all antidepressants studied. As C.J. Whittington and colleagues write, "Not publishing negative results undermines evidence-based medicine and puts millions of patients at risk for using ineffective or unsafe drugs."[10] According to a study published in *The New England Journal of Medicine*, "Selective reporting of clinical trial results may have adverse consequences for researchers, study participants, health care professionals, and patients."[11]

A more fair-minded dialogue is needed regarding the diagnosis of mental illness and depression in particular. While some favor and others oppose diagnosis and medical treatment, neither point of view should be dismissed. The diversity of clients' experiences of depression, as well as the situations, families, and cultures in which they live, calls for a diversity of understanding and treatments. Some lives are saved by diagnosis and psychopharmacology. Some clients find healing by discovering meaning in their symptoms. Some find relief and change through the help of a friend or healer. And many are assisted by others' efforts to make positive changes in their families, communities, and cultures. Finally, of course, some symptoms are best addressed by the blending of these and other approaches.

The Lie of Brian (Williams)

In 2015, Brian Williams, the longtime anchor of *NBC Nightly News*, was caught lying, padding his journalistic résumé with fabricated stories about the danger he faced while covering the Iraq War. Media pundits and others were aghast, asking questions like, "Why did he lie, given that he'd reached the top of his profession and earned a salary of millions?" Williams was suspended without pay, then reassigned to a lesser role on MSNBC.

Our culture is terribly naïve about psychology. We think that being rich and successful makes a person less desperate or more secure.

Instead of making Williams admit his lie and apologize for it, I would like to hear him say, "I tried to feel good about myself, but I never felt good enough. I constantly criticized myself. I inflated who I was, hoping that somehow the reflection back from my audience would overcome my inner sense of diminishment. Now I see that it never did and it never can."

Psychologist Julie Diamond, Ph.D., says, "Humans are exceptional liars, truth stretchers, story weavers, myth makers, and data ignorers."[1] This description applies not only to Brian Williams; many of us are subject to such fierce inner and outer criticism that we would do almost anything to feel good about ourselves.

Here are some of the most common ways we desperately attempt to boost our feelings about ourselves.

Some of us starve ourselves.

In fact, up to 24 million Americans suffer from eating disorders, which have the highest mortality rate of any mental illness.[2] Many of us try to dramatically change our bodies, to not be ourselves, so we will better reflect what our culture considers attractive.

Some of us are people pleasers.

We easily sacrifice our own truth because of fear of conflict or the need for affirmation. It's a twisted form of dishonesty, where we "will do almost anything to keep others in the dark about what is going on within."[3]

Some of us are addicted to trying to change ourselves.

We try to be less sensitive, even when we are being hurt; we push ourselves to be more productive, even when we need rest. We struggle to be less angry, more positive, less judgmental, less vulnerable. Many of us think we should become more spiritual, even if that involves rejecting who we really are. What powerful force keeps us speeding toward a kind of self-improvement that moves us further and further from our authentic selves?

Some of us do whatever we can to perform better.

It used to be only struggling students who cheated on exams, but not today. Each year, between 75-98% of surveyed college students admit to having cheated in high school. It starts even younger: Nearly 70% of students age 12 to 14 report cheating on exams, and 90% report copying homework.[4]

And how can we ignore the importance of performance in the bedroom, when sales for virility drugs like Viagra are over $5 billion each year?[5] Let's not kid ourselves that this is all about a medical condition. Men are trained to hide their vulnerability, to "inflate their résumé," at great psychological cost.

We all participate in creating a culture of denial.

We are complicit in creating an atmosphere that condones dishonesty. In a University of Southern California study, business students watched films of job interviews in which the applicant is confronted with having committed an infraction at a previous job and either apologizes for it or denies it. Participants then rated the trustworthiness of the applicant. Researchers concluded, "If you are guilty of an integrity-based violation and you apologize, that hurts you more than if you are dishonest and deny it."[6]

Further, we do our best to forget our racist history, especially toward Native Americans and people of color. As *Chicago Tribune* writer Jamelle Bouie notes, the new racism is to deny that racism exists.[7]

Additionally, climate-change denial has become a well-funded and coordinated effort designed to keep us from a truth that is more evident each year.

In short, we all work diligently to keep hard truths at bay.

Let's face it: *Keeping the truth from others, as well as ourselves, by trying to build ourselves up or denying anything that could bring us down, is a cultural malaise, an epidemic of perfectionism and self-hatred that lurks in the shadows. Many of us live in a prison of outer or inner criteria we will never meet.*

Moral outrage certainly has its place in the Brian Williams story. Clearly there are issues of journalistic integrity and the abuse of power, given his position. And issues of class, income inequality, race, and gender have a legitimate place in this conversation. But focusing only on moral outrage also serves as a kind of psychological defense system, keeping us blind to the dynamics that hide in our own psyches as well as in the consciousness of our culture.

Perhaps it's time for a psychological intervention, a coming out of the shadows for all of us. Perhaps we could all hold up placards that read: "Je suis Brian Williams"—I am Brian Williams. Now that would turn our world upside down; that would be a revolution I could sign up for.

4

Who Cheats? Who Lies?
Moving Beyond Lance Armstrong

Whe Lance Armstrong admitted to using performance-enhancing drugs and blood doping in an interview with Oprah Winfrey on January 17, 2013, much of the public responded with shock and outrage. After all, he cheated *and* he lied about it. People felt their contempt was 100% justified—Armstrong's actions were morally reprehensible, and, what's more, his public apology seemed inadequate and felt less than satisfying for many of us.

Who Cheats and Who Lies?

The truth about cheating and lying is that it's not just the Lance Armstrongs of the sports world, corrupt Wall Street executives, or those labeled "pathological" who are doing it. *Nearly all of us lie* at one point or another in our lives, and we do it far more regularly than we care to admit. Consider these alarming statistics on cheating, alone: 30 to 40% of Americans cheat on their taxes;[1] 30 to 60% of married people in the United States will engage in infidelity at some point during their marriage;[2] and 73% of all test takers, including prospective graduate students and teachers, agree that most students cheat at some point.[3]

As for lying? "Humans are exceptional liars, truth stretchers, story weavers, myth makers and data ignorers," says organizational consultant and facilitator Julie Diamond, Ph.D. She talks about the ways all of us spin the truth, exaggerate claims, and just plain lie all the time in our everyday lives. "When we read about ... Lance, we think it's something we wouldn't do. And here's what's scariest. It's not just something we could do but something we've probably already done, in our own way, in our own worlds and will do again. And we don't even remember doing it."[4] In short, cheaters and liars live a lot closer to home than many of us care to admit.

Co-creating Dishonesty:
Cultural and Systemic Causes of Dishonesty

Going further, it is critical to consider our culture's role in individual lying and cheating. Much of popular psychology holds individuals wholly responsible for themselves, including for their cheating and lying. From a larger perspective, however, individuals and social systems co-create problems, and the problems with one reflect problems with the other. While understanding this does not change individuals' responsibility, culpability, or need for help, it does expand our understanding of cheating and lying, making it more difficult for those who identify with social systems to throw stones without considering their own role in creating the cheating and lying of individuals.

For example, consider how mainstream culture exerts pressure on individual performance. As Lisa King writes in *Appalachian Chronicle*, "In 30 years, there has been a twenty-fold increase in the consumption of attention-deficit disorder medications. Four million children and teens in America are currently taking Ritalin."[5] One function of Ritalin is to *enhance students' performance*. Our educational focus has become so heavily weighted on good grades, rather than good education, that even students who say cheating is wrong still admit to cheating in order to get a good grade. Research about cheating among middle school children (ages 12–14) has shown they have increased motivation to cheat because of the increased focus on grades.[6] According to one recent survey of middle schoolers, two-thirds of respondents reported cheating on exams, while nine-tenths reported copying another's homework.[7]

Further, in 2002, CBS News reported that more than 50% of Americans drink coffee every day—up to four cups each. That meant more than 330 million cups per day and counting.[8] "We really want something that'll help us work harder, sharpen our minds, increase our sense of well-being, improve our performance," says Bennett Weinberg, author of *The Caffeine Advantage*.[9] In this case, it is coffee that enhances our performance. Another alarming example: A 2006 University of Minnesota study found that one in five young women had used diet pills by the age of twenty.[10] In effect, these diet drugs enhance our performance at achieving weight loss. Even in the bedroom, performance enhancement has become an epidemic. Annual sales to men for virility drugs like Viagra topped $5 billion in 2011.[11]

Before we get our backs up in judgment and horror, let's keep at least one eye on ourselves and the other on a mainstream culture that too readily scapegoats individuals rather than glance at its own shadow.

5

Upon the Murder of 20 Children and 6 Adults in Connecticut

Someone murdered 26 people this morning. Someone killed 20 innocent children. I can't help but think that it was not just innocents who were assaulted, but also innocence itself. And I can't help but think that our cultural innocence needs a wake-up call. While many say it is not time for philosophical or political discussion, I also know we can do something. We can act. We are not powerless.

In *The Fire Next Time,* James Baldwin wrote, "[I]t is not permissible that the authors of devastation should also be innocent. It is the innocence which constitutes the crime."[1] Are we, as a culture, too innocent? That is, are there too many people for whom this kind of violence seems like a rare event? Have we become too comfortable focusing our attention on the killers' psychology while neglecting to look at the epidemic nature of American violence? Have we become so accustomed to feeling powerless in the face of such horror that we learn to close our eyes to the violence all around us, as well as inside us?

Some twenty years ago, I read a newspaper story titled "Don't I Look Happy?" about a blond-haired, blue-eyed, smiling-faced teen who had murdered his parents and siblings. The article implied that the boy's appearance made it hard for anyone to predict that he had the potential to commit such violence. I remember another incident some years later, when friends and neighbors spoke to a television reporter about a high school shooting. They noted their surprise, saying that the shooter "always seemed like a happy boy." Is this need to look happy, to keep others smiling, feeding a dangerous form of innocence? I think so.

The forces of denial, of *a kind of collective amnesia*, urge us to keep ourselves "looking happy" rather than show our pain, suffering, and rage. We have become so invested in revealing only a narrow range of upbeat expressions that we don't notice the signs of violence, depression, and distress behind a happy demeanor. We are so accustomed to people telling us they're "fine" that we no longer trust the feelings that arise when things are not "fine." In other words, we no longer trust our distrust.

We don't see teenage girls on their knees throwing up in the toilet; instead, we admire their "nice" figures. We don't see businessmen endangering their health as they eat and drink their way to relaxation; instead, we view their excesses as a privilege of success. We don't notice the difference between gritted teeth and gleaming teeth, strained faces and composed faces, eyes that glare and eyes that glow. Our vision leans toward seeing the light but not what lies in the shadow. Our disconnectedness ensures that these aspects of people remain hidden.

It is time for many of us to come out with our deeper feelings and experiences—our pain, our sadness, our anger, our grief, our hurt. It is time for us to recognize these feelings in others. Otherwise, we collude in the violence by hiding. We collude by not seeing. Author and philosopher Cornel West said, "There is something about American folk. They're so obsessed with comfort, convenience, and contentment. It's just like living in a hotel where the lights are always on."[2] It's time to learn to see in the dark. It is my hope that psychology can help us do that.

6

Scapegoating, Stereotyping, and Projecting Won't Make Us Safer

This morning, as the news about Newtown played nonstop, there were many calls for improved mental health resources. I understand. We want answers. We want to prevent and protect. We want to throw our arms around those we love. We hope psychology will help us with this hunger.

However, I grow concerned as I witness the media looking, as usual, for a reason that lulls us back to a false sense of security—as if we could identify the reason one person hurts another and know that is not us or those directly around us. I grow concerned when people focus so much on the story and psychology of one individual, this time Adam Lanza, as if we all don't have work to do, as if we all don't have a certain responsibility—even if that is to care for ourselves, to notice the hurt, pain, and rage around us. I grow concerned when pundits throw around labels that could easily lead viewers to marginalize and even demonize a group of people whom they know little about.

I grow concerned because in moments of violence and trauma (be they hours, days, or even generations), the broader culture's unpsychological eye can easily project onto a person or group all the qualities it wants to split off from itself, thereby scapegoating those people and groups. This happens when folks project onto our gay brothers and sisters that they are dangerous to children. This happens when some project hostility onto our black brothers and sisters, as if violence is not epidemic among all racial groups in America.

The point is that stereotyping and projecting can give us a momentary feeling of security, but projecting onto others is another form of violence. It harms. Psychology should not be used to feed our hunger for security in this way. Psychology should make us more aware of our tendency to project and stereotype, and it should help us do no harm.

Consider the example of how some people use the label "autism." Some programs have claimed that Adam Lanza was autistic. Last night, CNN interviewed Dr. Sanjay Gupta, chief medical correspondent for the network. The reporter spoke about autism as a mental disorder and suggested that autism could lead to violence. Dr. Gupta quickly corrected the reporter, saying that autism is not a mental disorder but rather a neurodevelopmental disorder. He disabused the audience of the idea that autism could lead to this kind of violence.

But this morning, on *Meet the Press*, moderator David Gregory asked Pete Williams, NBC's justice correspondent, "Do we know why this happened? What do we know about Adam Lanza?" Mr. Williams responded by saying, among other things, "He had a mild form of autism." This time, nothing more was said, leaving viewers to connect autism with this kind of violence.

I don't think either David Gregory or Mr. Williams had any ill intent or were aware they were misleading people. And if this were simply a conversation between two people, I could let the ethical implications go. But this conversation was meant to educate millions of viewers; therefore, I believe there is an ethical obligation to protect groups from potential scapegoating.

In the words of the Autism Research Institute, "Autism is not a mental health disorder—it is a neurodevelopmental disorder. The eyes of the world are on this wrenching tragedy—with 1 in 88 now diagnosed, misinformation could easily trigger increased prejudice and misunderstanding."

In times of trauma, we all need to be careful and compassionate. As violent incidents occur, we need us to keep our eyes on potential scapegoating, projecting, and stereotyping. This is one way we can make the world a little safer.

7

Crazy About Gun Control

To my progressive friends (yes, you too, Piers Morgan):

As you listen to gun fanatic after gun lunatic talk about owning a Bushmaster and a high-capacity magazine or two, I understand your anger, your fury. Some of them are deluded, crazy, nuts.

These people are in something like a psychotic state—their position on guns is not held together by a web of logic and reason. Rather, it is held together by something much more powerful and less subject to change: their underlying psychology. Trying to change their point of view with a logical argument is like telling a lifelong smoker, "You know, smoking is not good for your health."

When you try to argue your friends out of their patterns, what does that make you? Well, it makes you as deluded, crazy, and as nuts as they are. Look, it's been more than 100 years since Freud announced to the Western world that there is something called the "unconscious," and that the unconscious is not only difficult to navigate, control, or tamper with, it also is *unconscious*. This means that the person whom you are trying to change doesn't have access to the reasons and powers that hold them to their position.

It is a kind of blindness that makes you persist in trying to change these folks with logic. This state of blindness is present not only because you are wildly disturbed by these people, but also because you are powerfully projecting onto them. The psychological remedy? You must withdraw and integrate that projection, which means you must discover how *you* are *them*. You must identify qualities that you dislike in them and see how you need some of those qualities yourself.

What kind of projection might you have on gun crazies? How might you need to be a little more like them psychologically? Consider the following:

A firm grip and steely resolve:

Think about it. Where might you be too understanding, too malleable, or too willing to listen to others? If your grip were firmer—if you were less wavering regarding your deepest convictions, feelings, needs, and desires—how would you proceed? More forcefully, more assertively, more directly? In short, withdrawing your projection means learning to stick to your own guns.

The capacity to shoot straight:

How direct are you with others around you—your employees, employers, friends, and family? With yourself? Speaking with sarcasm, beating around the bush, thinking others can't handle the truth, or assuming that direct communication won't help might just be signs of needing some firearms training. In short, withdrawing your projection may require that you aim your challenges and accusations of others with greater precision so that you hit your target.

Fully functioning defense systems:

It's not bad to defend yourself. It's not wrong to find your "inner attorney" when you feel wrongly or unjustly criticized or accused. When you are feeling nervous or insecure, especially with someone who has more power than you (e.g., your boss, your spouse, the law, parents, experts, or those whose praise you seek), you may still need to follow your own truth regardless of the consequences.

On the other hand, when you find that you are genuinely insecure, you may need to own up to it—to drop your stiff upper lip and hard exterior and show some vulnerability. If you can't be open to your own insecurity, your defense mechanisms cut you off from yourself and others at times. In short, you need to consciously decide when to remove your bulletproof vest because your position is already shot through with holes.

Finally, in service of being a firm, straight-shooting, vulnerability-risking therapist, let me say it plain: These gun nuts are crazy, but so are you. It's time for less logic and more "psycho-logic." While waking up the gun fanatics may not be an easy task, it doesn't mean you have to bask unconsciously in your own projections and mini-psychoses.

It's time to stop beating our heads against the brick wall of another gun fanatic's belief system—which we make even more impenetrable by imbuing it with the power of our own projections. Let's withdraw this power and learn to use our psychological weapons and defenses where we can make a difference: with ourselves, our friends, our families, and our local communities.

Now that you know the psychological truth, what can you do about it? Simply put, you have to empathize with them. You have to find the gun-crazy, arms-carrying, home-protecting, government-fighting, unflinching, unchangeable, "You will have to pull it out of my cold, dead hands" part of yourself. How do you do this? Try the quick exercise below. I'll help by joining you and describing my experiences in italics. Here's how:

1.) Imagine that you hold in your hand a collection of rights that are under political and legislative assault by a group of Tea Party fanatics who want to overturn Roe v. Wade, undermine the public-education system, and cut programs for the poor. Feel your reaction and locate it within your body. *I can feel my reaction in my teeth, jaw, loins, stomach muscles, thighs, and fingers.*

2.) Let your hand form a grip with a force consistent with your desire to hold on to these rights. *I have a very tight fist in my left hand, my dominant hand, and I can feel the nails begin to make an indent into the palm of my hand.*

3.) Forget about what you are holding on to and why you are holding so tightly. Just "become" that grip, that force, that fist, that power. What kind of person, substance, or animal do you imagine you are? *I feel like a large stone; outside I am immovable, but inside I am quiet, calm, and unaffected.*

4.) How or where do you need to be more like that in your life? *Actually, I can be far too open to others' viewpoints and opinions. As a stone, I would not listen to others as much; I would pay more attention to my own inner voice and follow that more religiously.*

5.) In what way does that mean becoming, in a psychological way, a little bit more like the gun-crazy folks? *I don't listen to others; I am not moved by their logic; I follow myself "religiously" regardless of the fact that it doesn't consider others.*

Enjoy your new, more steadfast self. And, if you can, imagine that the gun crazies have a very loose grip on themselves and therefore need to hold on even tighter to their own viewpoints, perspective, and religion—just like you do.

8

Upon the Boston Marathon Bombings

"**K**eep calm and carry on." "Resume your normal life as quickly as possible." "Nothing will stop us from staying the course." "Let's fight the fear and terror—let's have a War on Terror."

Many Americans pride themselves on not being deterred or diverted from their tasks, goals, and everyday lives. But when traumatic events don't give us pause and inspire critical thinking and psychological reflection, this perseverance becomes a form of denial. This is my concern regarding our response to violent interruptions of our routines, like the one we experienced after the Boston Marathon bombings of April 15, 2013.

Often individuals come to therapy with the goal of making changes in their lives because their usual methods aren't working. In fact, these old approaches are part of the problem and therefore cannot be part of the cure. But therapy isn't always enough to change fundamental behaviors, and people often continue to assert their primary beliefs and values until enough love or trauma intervenes.

Couples have a similar dynamic. They tend to deny their true feelings—even the damage they cause themselves and each other—in order to perpetuate their unresolved familial and cultural stories until trauma or the next generation breaks the cycle.

And finally, groups, communities, and nations also practice an almost pathological perseverance of strategies and attitudes, including obviously prejudicial and hypocritical ways of relating to people of different races, ethnicities, and genders until the spirit of the times confronts these old ways and derails them.

Why are we so unwilling to engage in self-reflection? Are we so without love and respect for ourselves that we cannot bear our own criticism? Are we so insecure that we cannot acknowledge our fear and insecurity? Must we, almost pathologically, invest more and more on our *inner defense budgets* until we realize that the resources needed for our deeper understanding and growth have been totally sacrificed for a life of imagined security and false confidence?

In his well-loved poem "Keeping Quiet," Pablo Neruda wrote:

> If we were not so single-minded
> about keeping our lives moving,
> and for once could do nothing,
>
> perhaps a huge silence
> might interrupt this sadness
> of never understanding ourselves
> and of threatening ourselves with death.

I hope that we can stop for a moment. That we can change. Not because we are worthy of being hated by Chechen terrorists, but out of the moral and spiritual power of our eldership—a sense that we are psychologically mature enough to make meaning and transformation out of our suffering instead of creating more denial and more powerful defense systems.

9

Racism on Trial:
Reflections on the Prosecution of George Zimmerman for the Murder of Trayvon Martin

The 2013 trial of George Zimmerman for the shooting death of Trayvon Martin captured the media's attention. Television, print media, and blogs detailed every minute of testimony from witnesses, comments from judges, and macerations of attorneys, as well as a wide range of opinions about what actually happened the night of the shooting and what the result of the trial should be.

While I was happy to see this level of transparency and public interest and investment in the case, I am concerned that the focus on the details of this particular case in fact obscured the background feelings, history, and experiences that fueled much of the interest. These background elements relate to what W. E. B. Du Bois called "the color line," or "the relation between the darker and lighter races." On both sides of that line are feelings of anger, hurt, resentment, and misunderstanding.

The racial divide is apparent in the tens of thousands of comments that were posted in response to almost every online article about the Zimmerman trial. Many of these comments appeared on the surface to be logical and rational but were in fact loaded with subtext and fueled by a longstanding racial animosity, echoing America's racial history of injury, injustice, and resentment and expressing feelings that are palpable on the streets today.

About George Zimmerman:

Some say Zimmerman is a wannabe cop, a hateful liar, and a near-sociopath in his lack of concern for his murder of a teenager. Others say he is an innocent victim and a Good Samaritan who made his neighbors' lives safer.

About Trayvon Martin:

Some say he was a Skittles-carrying, college-bound, loving teenager in whose eyes one can see complete innocence. Others see a drug-using, troublemaking, predatory "gangsta" raised in a culture of violence, hunting for prey on streets he didn't belong on, and deserving of the fate he brought upon himself.

About Trayvon's mother:

Some say that Sybrina Fulton was a woman of low morals, a liar, and an inadequate mother to Trayvon who feigned her feelings about her son for improper gain. Others say she is a loving, grieving, forthright, and heroic woman victimized by the defense team and the media.

About the judge and jury:

Some say that the judge was in the tank for Trayvon and always stood against the defense's objections and motions, while others say that the all-white jury was in the tank for Zimmerman and would find him not guilty regardless of the facts.

About the legal system:

Some say that there is no way a white man can get a fair trial in this country when the alleged "victim" is an African-American male. Others say that a black victim will never be valued as highly as a white victim and that black defendants are more likely to be suspected, arrested, convicted, and penalized.

About Zimmerman's guilt or innocence:

Some say that Zimmerman's acquittal calls the entire American justice system into question. Others say the justice system functioned exactly as it should have in evaluating the facts and rendering the proper verdict.

About the role of race in this case:

Some declare that the trial was about "black racism" biased against Zimmerman, and that he was tried because of a politically correct legal system and "lynched" in the media. Others say that a young black male was profiled, pursued, and killed because of his race and presented to a jury who would never "get" Trayvon or sympathize with him, his mother, or his friend Rachel Jeantel.

Regardless of your opinions about George Zimmerman and Trayvon Martin, we must not ignore the underlying conversation —a heated, potent, and critical discussion about race and racism. The debate is about American history and our awareness of that history. The debate is about how far America has come, or not come, from its racist past. The debate is about who is responsible today for the psychic, economic, and social conditions of many black folks.

This discussion goes on in the Supreme Court, where a five-four decision struck down an essential element of the Voting Rights Act of 1965. It goes on in the back-and-forth commentary between MSNBC and Fox News. It fuels many of the hundreds of thousands of comments on social media. It informs our judgments, assumptions, feelings, and perceptions.

The verdict of this debate: *Regardless of where you stand, the racial divide in America is alive.* The wound is festering; the anger and resentment is hot; the differences in viewpoints are potent and real; and the capacity to really listen, understand, or step into the other's shoes is a rarity.

The long, terrible night of racial injustice is not over, and the wounds from that history are far from healed. The Zimmerman verdict puts salt on that wound. And it hurts. I do not say this as a declaration about Zimmerman; I say this as an assertion about my country.

Langston Hughes cautioned that a dream deferred may explode. Please be careful, friends; the darkness around us is deep.

In Honor of Maya Angelou:
This Caged Bird Sang and Sang

Maya Angelou was raped as a child. When she visited her aunt and uncle, she was frightened to tell them about the rapist for fear her uncle would hurt this man. But she decided to use her voice; she decided to tell.

Some time afterwards, a sheriff knocked on the door to report that the man had been found dead. Maya, age eight, concluded that she was responsible. To protect others from the power of her voice, which she believed not only killed the man who raped her but also could kill anyone, she decided not to speak.[1] And she did not speak for more than five years.[2]

Of course, I don't think she killed this man. But I do think her voice had immense power. Anyone who listened to her couldn't help but be profoundly moved. The unfolding and life-giving power of that voice would influence the course of millions of lives.

In her silence, she created an alchemical chamber where the power and absolute beauty of her voice unfolded and flowered. Her grandmother, whom she called "Mama," never tried to correct Maya or "heal" her from her wound. Instead, Mama kept telling Maya that she would be a great teacher someday. Mama knew something that very few would even consider: that the soul, spirit, and nature of this young girl were transforming and needed to be held in a radical faith and love.

Maya suffered great insult during her years of not speaking. She communicated with others by writing and was criticized and mocked for it. She spent much time under Mama's porch, feeding on poetry by authors black and white.

One day, six years after Maya had lapsed into silence, Mama said, "You'll never appreciate those words until you hear them rolling off your own lips."[3] She took Maya to church to speak before the congregation. Maya let some poetry pass through her lips, but they were not the words of a black poet as most would have expected. She said:

> When, in disgrace with fortune and men's eyes,
> I all alone beweep my outcast state,
> And trouble deaf heaven with my bootless cries,
> And look upon myself and curse my fate,
> Wishing me like to one more rich in hope,
> Featured like him, like him with friends possess'd,
> Desiring this man's art and that man's scope,
> With what I most enjoy contented least;
> Yet in these thoughts myself almost despising,
> Haply I think on thee, and then my state,
> Like to the lark at break of day arising
> From sullen earth, sings hymns at heaven's gate;
>> For thy sweet love remember'd such wealth brings
>> That then I scorn to change my state with kings.

This is Sonnet 29 by William Shakespeare. When asked why she recited a poem by Shakespeare and not a black poet, Maya said, "I knew that was written for me."

Maya knew, as a black girl, a silent child, what it meant to be "in disgrace with fortune and men's eyes"; I'm sure that often, she "alone bewept her outcast state." But she also knew that nature made her, even in her trauma, more than a king.

The first time I saw Dr. Angelou, she was in her sixties. She told the story of her rape. Some counselors in the audience commented privately that she needed to let this part of her story go, but I was inspired that she didn't just "heal it away." Instead, she made it into something. Life, Mama, and Maya made that story into something gloriously human with the potential we all have to make the deepest humanity out of our pain and suffering. I can hear her saying, "I am a human being; nothing human can be alien to me."[4]

The next time I saw her, she was about 76 years old. She asked to be introduced as "Dr. Maya Angelou." She had earned her doctorate degree and had received many honorary doctorates; she spoke seven languages. She said something that amazed me: that it was not easy for her to ask others to use the title "doctor" in reference to her. Mainstream America had no trouble seeing her as a poet, author, and dancer, but to see her as a doctor—many still had to get over their prejudices to be comfortable calling a black woman "doctor."

This is still true. Here was one of the grandest intelligences America had to offer. Here was a black woman six feet tall, wearing heels and a sleeveless blouse, standing before thousands who came to hear her speak, and still she was growing into her full self, her full powers. What a model!

The last time I saw Dr. Angelou she told a story of a white woman who approached her after one of her public appearances. The woman said that her daughter had been suicidal but changed the course of her life after hearing Dr. Angelou speak. And then the woman did something unexpected. She said that she was surprised to learn that this influence on her daughter's life looked like her—a black woman.

My eyes teared; my gut cringed. How would this model of humanity respond? I imagined she would see this woman for the ignorant child she was. Instead, Maya said that she went home and cried much of the weekend. She cried, even though many of us think we shouldn't "take things personally," "suffer fools gladly," etc. She cried, and that meant that I could also. I was in law school at the time and in my early forties. I cried many evenings after class. Maya told me it was okay.

In an interview with Dr. Cornel West, Dr. Angelou told a story from when she worked on the set of the film *Poetic Justice*. A fight ensued between two men and threatened to become violent. People on the set backed off to protect themselves. She stepped in, put her hands on one of the men, and said, "Let me speak to you. Let me talk to you. Do you know you're the best we have? Do you know we don't have anybody better than you? Do you know everybody has paid for you, and they're all dead?"[5] The man started to cry and she walked him away from others so he would not be ashamed of his tears. She didn't know at the time that the man was Tupac Shakur.

When asked in an interview years later why she did that, Dr. Angelou said that sometimes we have to put our hands on another person and remind them how precious they are, that they are the best we have.

In honor of Dr. Maya Angelou, may I say in my own voice, a voice empowered by hers, you are the best we have; each of us is the best we have.

Beyond a Popular Psychology:
Remembering the Shadow

Into the Dark:
A Psychology of Soul, Shadow, and Diversity

I don't know about you, but I can't stand to see one more article or book titled "5 Elements of Success," "7 Keys to Happiness," "6 Steps to Healing," ad infinitum. Not that these writings are without merit, but let's face it—they often dumb us down. Of course it's seductive to be given The Answer, especially when it's the answer to everything we've ever wanted. But at what cost? What gets left behind?

To me, these teachings leave out our depth and soul. They fail to account for the humans on the planet who have few options, including many women, children, and people of color. They also leave out our authentic lives and the crosses we must bear to follow our callings, our shadows, our death, our decay. Perhaps most urgently, they ignore that which we share and which often brings us to the heart of the matter: our need for love.

Depth and Soul:

Our unique natures, our struggles, and the paths of our healing and happiness are incredibly nuanced. Just looking at people's dreams, you see that some folks need to learn tenderness while others need to learn ferocity. Some people need to learn to jump, take off, and fly while others need to learn to be more grounded.

Some need to learn to set clearer boundaries while others need to learn to be more open and less defensive. Some need to stand up for themselves, and others need to let go. Some need to find more energy in their lives while others need to drop down, relax, and chill out.

As we learn and grow, unfolding our lives becomes less general and more finely tuned to our individual natures. Carl Jung called this "individuation," a word that comes from the Latin *individuus,* meaning "undivided" or "individual." Insofar as individuality embraces our innermost and incomparable uniqueness, it also implies becoming one's own self. Jung therefore translates "individuation" as "coming to selfhood" or "self-realization."

Diversity:

In a world that needs to learn about (and from) its diversity, we need a psychology that mirrors and promotes that diversity. Mainstream psychology is created for middle-class western white folk. Worse, this psychology often promotes a normativity that has more to do with socialization than wellness.

Take, for example, the idea that everything arises out of choice —that we need to make choices to actualize a better life for ourselves and take responsibility for the choices we have made. While this outlook may contain a deep spiritual truth, something I will not debate here, much of the planet (including much of the United States) is comprised of people who are seriously marginalized and underprivileged, such that major areas of their lives are determined by factors beyond their individual control. In fact, some of the most significant traumatic events (trauma being an issue that any worthy psychology ought to address) have been created by the victimization of whole groups of people, from African Americans and Jews to women and our gay brothers and sisters.

A psychology that does not speak to (or at least note its relative neglect of) those "with their backs against the wall" perpetrates an injury against these groups via its complicit silence on this issue. This neglect hurts everyone, as we all contain a profound inner diversity as well as a diversity of styles, gifts, and natures.

Shadow:

Much advice in this simplified psychology is biased toward what is considered positive, light, or happy—ignoring the power, beauty, and love found in the shadow. As the renowned African-American scholar Cornel West said, "We live in a hotel civilization ... in which people are obsessed with comfort, contentment, and convenience, where the lights are always on."[1]

If we promote a psychology that equates health with light, happiness, lack of physical symptoms, and conflict-free relationships, we dismiss and deny the truths and the important growth that can be found in the blues, in sickness, in conflict, in the shadows. For example, anger is often considered a symptom to be remedied, but anger can be a great source of power. Sometimes people need to stand up for themselves, resist inner criticism, speak out against injustice, and make sustainable change by using righteous anger to right wrongs.

Also, while depression is often viewed as a symptom to be fixed through medication, difficult times can unearth profound truths. People with depression might rediscover values they had left behind or gain insight into difficulties they had not identified. Depression can be a powerful invitation to look deeper into the self, a space free of the ambitions and activities of daily life, to ask the underlying questions they have been ignoring for so long.

Death and Decay:

Further hidden in the shadows are our death, decay, and illness. Mainstream perspectives are invariably biased towards growing, living, increasing. But death is part of life's bargain and, as I learned in my time as a hospice worker, is not made more graceful and marvelous by being viewed as the enemy to be beaten. When we view growing old as something to combat, illness as something to cure, death as something to push away, we fail to embrace their power and beauty. In fact, consciously befriending the dying process, whether during illness or when death is imminent, can be one of the most fruitful, heart-opening, spiritual, and intimate experiences of our lives. The loss of our everyday lives often opens the door to our most essential selves.

Authenticity:

Many of us must bear a cross before we can live in accord with our authentic nature. That cross may manifest as illness, conflict, broken relationships, addictions, and difficult emotional states, all of which may be exacerbated by isolation and living outside the norm. Those who are called to live closely to their authentic nature need appreciation—even celebration—not marginalization and dismissal through simplistic psychological notions and paradigms that equate these challenges with inferiority, lack of virtue, or lack of psychological or spiritual development.

Humanity:

What does it mean to be human? Does it mean being happy, successful, and symptom-free? Or does it mean living fully and wholly, engaging in what Zorba the Greek called "the full catastrophe"? Projecting what is called "illness" and "negativity" onto others prevents us from seeing that it is not they that are the "wretched of the earth," it is *we*. We are the starving child, the raped woman, the Jew in the concentration camp, the lonely widower, the maimed soldier. And we are also the Nazi, the rapist. ...

As Maya Angelou said, "I am a human being; nothing human can be alien to me." *This is the new paradigm for psychology.* Unlike many of the current psychologies, it does not promote, support, or coerce conformity and normality. Instead, it promotes diversity and a deep private and public love for who we really are. We will be healed not when we rid ourselves and the world of symptoms, tears, and violence, but when we look upon these through new eyes, eyes that know *this is me, this is you, and we are all in this together.* It is my sincere belief that these new eyes will bring healing in ways that many of the efforts to change and improve the self can never do. They will bring healing through love.

2

Building and Repairing Trust: Keys to Sustainable Relationships

Why is trust such a popular topic for writers and readers alike? Simply put, because all of us have had our trust betrayed.

Trust is a kind of agreement, whether spoken or unspoken, that people will treat us a certain way. When someone betrays us, they violate that agreement, causing an emotional or physical injury.

Lying and deceiving is perhaps the most basic form of betrayal. It defies a spoken or unspoken rule that we will be treated honestly, and is therefore emotionally hurtful.

For example, monogamous couples agree to not have sexual relationships with others. Having an affair violates that agreement and almost always emotionally injures the partner; thus, it is a betrayal of trust. In another example, physically or verbally assaulting a person not only causes injury but also violates the unspoken agreement that we don't harm each other; thus, it is a betrayal of trust. These betrayals, when not addressed, can create wounds and scars that limit intimacy in relationships.

How Can Trust Be Repaired and Rebuilt?

The first step is to *become fully aware of the nature and extent of the hurt* you feel. If your hurt is dismissed, minimized, or denied—by yourself or others—the wound is likely to fester and it is unlikely trust will be repaired. To ensure that this does not happen, ask yourself the following questions: How deep is the hurt/pain you suffer? Does the betrayal trigger earlier hurts that exacerbate the pain and suffering? Does the hurt linger for days, months, or even years?

Second, the person or group who betrayed you must really see and acknowledge the hurt. Apologies like "I'm sorry you feel that way" or "I didn't mean to hurt you" often stop the healing process before the hurt is really looked at and properly acknowledged. Rather than offering insufficient forms of apology, the one who betrayed you must acknowledge the injury, take some responsibility for the hurt, and show a feeling reaction commensurate with the hurt (such as remorse, compassion, or agitation). When there is no real acknowledgment or feeling response, you may rightly feel that the person "doesn't get it," and the trust will not be repaired.

Does repairing trust require a promise to not hurt you again? While sometimes this is necessary, if this promise is not accompanied by a real acknowledgment and proper response, the promise will carry little weight and, in all likelihood, will not be kept. These insufficient promises are almost always built on the hope that the one who betrayed you can control themselves, or that you can somehow control them, as opposed to a deeper sense of love and respect.

Going Deeper: Living a Life Where Betrayal Is Inevitable

Trying to create a life where betrayal can never occur can cause us to withdraw and be too wary of taking risks. It can insulate us from being truly alive. *Betrayal is inevitable.* Sometimes it is as simple as one person agreeing to be a certain kind of partner and later discovering that they have needs and desires they can no longer suppress or accommodate. For example, if you agree to financially support your family but later learn that pursuing your artistic life is more important than you realized, you might have to revise your promise. Or, if you agreed to always listen to your partner, you may find that you have suppressed the need to voice your own opinions, needs, or feelings for too long and can no longer listen in the same way. Or, if you agreed to "always be there" for your partner and then find that you have a deeper need for friendships than you initially realized, you might spend more time with friends than your partner expects.

Also, we all have a shadow—qualities, needs, and capacities that are not fully known to us. These shadowy aspects can be hurtful, in part because they are unconscious and express themselves without our care, sensitivity, or sense of responsibility. It may be our anger, vengeance, selfishness, jealousy, resentment, fear, or meanness; or, it could be our need to feel free, important, powerful, or even beautiful. Trying to make these qualities go away or promising not to ever express them is simply impossible. This cannot be overstated: *we cannot promise to not be something that is a part of us, especially when we are barely conscious of these parts.* Trying to control our own or others' shadows is suppressive and destined to fail. In fact, it often leads to an explosion of these qualities in unexpected and more problematic ways.

If Betrayal Is Unavoidable, How Can Your Relationship Thrive?

First, get to know yourself and your partner deeply—especially those aspects you may not like. At the beginning of relationships, we all ignore our partner's shadow and hide our own undesirable side. But as the relationship progresses, it is important to make a conscious effort to explore, discuss, and be open to learning about these parts of ourselves and others.

Second, begin to "trust" that you and your partner really have those qualities and will sometimes express them. Promising not to express these qualities cannot be trusted! Trust, in this case, is not built on the hope or promise of not being hurt, but built on a kind of deep honesty of who you and the other person really are.

Finally, learn, over time, that you can respond and take another step in the relationship even after hurts and betrayals have occurred. This requires a new kind of trust—the trust in yourself to be aware of your hurts and express them to your partner. Essentially, you are saying, "I trust that there are times you will hurt me and I will hurt you. I even trust that sometimes this hurt will be a breach of an agreement we have. However, I also trust that we can take steps to address these hurts and breaches and turn the process, over time, into a strengthening of our relationship."

Of course, some breaches are so great that they can never be fully repaired. I am not suggesting, for instance, that a person who is physically violated should "work it out." You alone will know if the bridge of relationship is irreparably broken. You must trust your own wisdom to recognize this and act accordingly.

3

Six Reasons Not to Forgive — Not Yet

I readily admit that there is a moral imperative to forgive; it is clear that forgiveness can be a powerful force of healing and reconciliation.

However, it troubles me that so many blog posts, articles, books, and spiritual slogans treat forgiveness as a panacea for healing hurt and pain and "moving on" to a happier life, giving no thought to the situations and stages of injury where this advice is not helpful. In fact, much of this counsel is downright offensive, suggesting that if we can't forgive, we are dwelling on the past, holding on to grudges, filled with retribution and revenge, addicted to adrenaline, marrying our victimhood, recoiling in self-protection, or poisoning ourselves with resentment.

These assumptions and judgments not only dismiss real pain, but they also discourage intelligent analysis of the traumas that many people and groups experience. Further, these statements can *shame* people, making them think something is wrong with a healing process where forgiveness may not be the first (or second or third) step. The truth is that many people don't forgive because it is not *time* to forgive—and proceeding at their own pace can be empowering, intelligent, and *worthy.* Simply put, it is alarming how un-psychological many psychologists can be; forgiveness is *not* the best medicine for all people all the time.

In fact, it may even make a person sick.

One person I spoke with said it well: "When I was at my most precarious in my attachment to this life, I knew my new therapist was a keeper when I began to reveal the true history of what had been done to me, and she did *not* speak of forgiveness."

1. Urging forgiveness ignores the fact that anger naturally arises as a response to hurt and often needs to be integrated, not rooted out like some bacteria-borne illness.

Anger has a raw power that can be integrated, a power that can help people stand up for themselves, build self-confidence, and avoid future injury. In fact, research shows that forgiving too readily can erode self-respect[1], causing greater relationship problems and leading people to accept poor treatment from their partners.[2] The point is that claiming some of our anger can be healing and productive.

Listen to the compelling voice of one woman: "I have walked away from the Big Forgive in my life. Every time I saw some version of that sermon—'Forgive in order to heal!' or 'You're only hurting yourself if you don't forgive!'—I debated what this meant for the family member who sexually abused me. I finally said, 'Screw it.' Sometimes I'm angry; sometimes I'm at peace."

2. Encouraging people to let go of anger prematurely is suppressive and harmful.

When anger and vengeful feelings are suppressed, they get internalized. Why is this a problem? Internalized anger often shows up as powerful, painful, even crippling inner criticism, putting salt on the very wound we hope to heal. Also, suppressed anger can lead to depression, relationship difficulties, and myriad health issues such as high blood pressure, heart problems, headaches, and digestive upset.

3. Counseling people to forgive a recent injury risks dismissing their pain.

It may seem obvious that telling a person to forgive a recent injury can be insensitive. However, many offer this advice cavalierly, without regard to timing. The truth is, people have their own way of dealing with hurt and betrayal, and their timing depends upon the severity of the injury, their natural process, and the reactions of others in whom they confide their pain. Promoting forgiveness without sensitivity to these factors can be hurtful and shaming. When is an injury "still recent"? Sometimes days, sometimes months, sometimes years.

4. Advising forgiveness can ignore the value of confronting an offender.

What if I told you that forgiving too readily makes it more likely that those who hurt you will hurt you again? This is exactly what professor James K. McNulty found: that partners who forgave their partners easily were almost twice as likely to be mistreated soon afterward.

Further, confronting your offender may not only make your life better but it can also make the world safer for others. Bullying, abuse, assault, and discrimination can be abated, if not eliminated, by confrontation.

In the words of one person I spoke with: "Calling someone out on what they did to hurt others is one way to make changes in the world. So many injustices happen because no one says anything about them."

5. Is advising forgiveness appropriate?
Depends upon who is asking whom to forgive.

Here's a no-brainer: If someone abuses you and then tells you to forgive and let go, they don't have your best interests at heart. Or when the person counseling forgiveness has an emotional or financial connection with the one who injured you, you have good reason to hesitate before trusting this counsel. For example, one parent may ask you to forgive the other, a religious authority may suggest you forgive the clergy, a politician may ask you to forgive their own indiscretions, or a person you know may sympathize more with the injurer than with you. Essentially, where conflicts of interest are present, beware and slow down before trying to forgive.

6. Advising forgiveness, or "letting go," to groups of people who have suffered sustained injustice is highly suspect.

So many blog posts and articles preach forgiveness while failing to consider the injuries created by sustained social prejudice and marginalization. They discuss forgiveness as if it were only an individual process—one person forgiving another. In a way, conventional thinking about forgiveness ignores some of the most profound injuries of our time regarding race, gender, and other issues of diversity:

1.) First, it dismisses the great strides that have been made by women, people of color, LGBTQ people, disabled folks, and other marginalized groups when people turned their anger into social action. They didn't only practice letting go. They *harnessed* their rage and vengeance to lift their arms and voices for the benefit of many, and for the development of America's democratic project.

2.) Second, it ignores the fact that powerful prejudices *still exist* and that these injuries are not just a thing of the past. Shall we forgive an abuser in the middle of their abusive act?

3.) Finally, this counsel often comes from people or groups who either have more power or a vested interest in not looking in the mirror at their culpability and not redressing social ills. It leads one to ask: Are the proponents of this advice out of touch with the history of injuries perpetrated over generations, a history that is still living today? Are they, however unconsciously, hoping to absolve their guilt without consequences? Clearly, we can't be outraged by racism in Ferguson and then promote forgiveness and letting go as the only door to healing injury and injustice. William Grier and Price Cobbs highlighted this problem in their seminal work *Black Rage*, declaring, "The gravest danger we see is that unscrupulous people may use psychotherapy with blacks as a means of social control, to persuade the patient to be satisfied with his lot."[3]

It's true that forgiveness can be a crucial stage in the healing process. But please, before counseling forgiveness, be aware of the power and diversity of injuries as well as the nature of the person or group you are counseling. If we counsel forgiveness as a general practice, we turn a blind eye to so many, and we may unwittingly shame those for whom forgiveness is not the next right step.

4

Understanding Stress:
Beyond Reduction, Management, and Coping

Sometimes it appears as if "stress" is the cause for all that ails us. Every day, I hear people say "I'm so stressed," and stress is currently one of the most written-about areas of psychology. Feeling physically ill? Stress. Not sleeping? Stress. Fighting with your partner? Stress. Forgetting things? Stress. Feeling depressed? Stress. Eating, drinking, drugging too much? Stress.

The literature is rife with research strengthening this assumption, showing that stress can make us ill, weaken our immune systems, make us emotionally volatile, damage our relationships, cause us to use and abuse substances, make us age more quickly, impair our memory, keep us awake at night, bring on anxiety and depression, and quash our libido.[1] It wouldn't be too much to say that stress kills.

Not to worry. The cure is waiting to descend on anyone open to getting help from friends, bloggers, authors, counselors, and more. I am reminded of that old adage, "If all we have is a hammer, everything looks like a nail." Well, if the concept of "stress" dominates our diagnosis and understanding of everything that ails us, we are sure to find indicators of stress everywhere we look. Now we just need "The Cure" for stress and all our problems will be solved.

So-called "cures" are indeed prevalent. We are told to unwind with friends, sleep more, change our diets, laugh, think positively, get massages, meditate, take more quiet time, exercise, pray, practice yoga, listen to relaxation tapes, and breathe more deeply.[2] So how come we're all still so stressed?

The advice from the literature is essentially the same, telling us how to calm down, relax, and take it easy. This counsel is packaged as "stress reduction," "stress management," and "coping with stress"—all phrases that assume the stress itself has no usefulness and is not in need of deeper understanding and transformation. Stress is to be gotten rid of like an illness.[3]

This bias, however, has serious drawbacks, causing us to misunderstand the background psychological processes and dynamics of stress.

First, *some stress needs to be amplified rather than relieved, and the power behind the stressor needs to be integrated*. For example, while teaching a psychology class to massage school students, I asked them what they would do with the tension in my shoulders. One after another they came over to me and rubbed my shoulders in order to relax them. In response to some students, I eased my shoulders, allowing them to drop; for other students I moved my shoulders around to stretch them and push them up against their hands. For people who would simply automatically relax, their interventions were just right. But there is another kind of person whose tension indicates that they have energy in their shoulders and bodies that they need to use in order to later relax.

The same is true for people in more psychological areas of their lives. Some need to relax, take it easy, or be gentler with themselves. Others need to push back and really use the power and force that is in them. For the latter kind of person, stress reduction in the form of trying to take it easy and relax will not work. The stress will simply re-arise because the person needs to learn to use the energy in their system instead of letting it go.

Second, *some stress is caused by a background neglect of something —a calling, a project, or a passion*. For example, consider a client who had a big dream for his life, but after entering a committed relationship began to let go of his dream so that he could be more present and available to his partner. This man described himself as incredibly stressed out. It would be easy for most people to quickly jump in and try to help him manage and reduce his stress. However, pregnant in the energy of what he called "stress" was a power and desire to go back to his dream and work to fulfill it.

This principle holds for many of us. Most people are not free to be as powerful, direct, and intense as they really are. Their energy becomes somatized and psychologized, meaning that it feels like physical tension and often gets labeled as "stress." My client didn't need to relax more—he needed to use the tension inside him to resist a patriarchal role in his relationship and instead take on the heavy lifting of his deeper dreams. Relieving his stress would not be sustainable because what he considered "stress" was actually something in his life that was not getting attention.

Third, *stress reduction and stress management may not be the best ways to address the specific issues that people are actually stressed about* (the content of their stress). For example, people report being the most stressed by lack of sleep and concern about their weight.[4] Is stress reduction and management the best medicine for these ills? As for concerns about sleep, we know that at least 40 million Americans each year suffer from chronic, long-term sleep disorders, and an additional 20 million experience occasional sleeping problems.[5] Insomnia tends to increase with age and affects about 40% of women and 30% of men.[6] It is often the major disabling symptom of an underlying medical disorder.[7] Will advising people to relax, cope, or reduce their stress help them sleep? Most experts in this area recommend consistent sleep schedules, watching what we eat and drink, creating nighttime rituals, exercising during the day, and not taking naps. Stress can be important, but it's rarely on top of the list.[8]

What about weight worries? Will telling people to relax offer any solace? First, it is important to note that people only sustain weight loss about 5% to 10% of the time.[9] And research indicates that people, especially women, are regularly cruel to their bodies.[10] In my own research, I have learned that loving one's body is not about relaxing or taking it easy; rather, it is a confrontation with cultural pressures and norms and a call to making real changes in relationships, work, and more. Telling people to relax will likely be ineffective and is a superficial response to the complex dilemma people face. Instead, we need to either change the culture's pressures and criticisms about body image or help people make profound changes in their lives.

Finally, much of what is written about stress fails to address the stress suffered by people who wrestle societal discrimination and marginalization. They search for articles about stress, but don't see their problems reflected. As such, conventional notions of stress contribute to their marginalization, creating further distress.

For example, blacks are stressed by biased employment systems and law enforcement systems and have a history of trauma carried over for generations.[11] Racism "has negative psychological consequences for African Americans such as increased symptoms of anxiety, depression, and post-traumatic stress."[12] There exists a similar neglect of the societal discrimination suffered by Native Americans, especially Native American females.

Simply put, we need a model that goes beyond stress management and reduction and "situates [stress] within the larger context of... colonized people."[13] We need a model that goes beyond the coping strategies of the individual to include changes needed in the wider culture, a model where the stresses of marginalized people can be reflected and affirmed.

I have no doubt that some people who are stressed need help to cope with and manage their stress. I have benefited from this advice at times. However, this orientation can dumb down our understanding. We need more critical and psychological reflection so that deep and powerful causes of suffering aren't brushed away by quick-fix answers like, "Don't worry, be happy" or "Relax, take it easy, let go—and don't get so stressed out."

5

Three Things to Learn from Failure

Sometimes we succeed—we achieve our intended goals and ends. Sometimes we fail and are left with the material and psychological fallout. Most of the counsel about failure essentially says, "Failure can be a good thing," "Look at the bright side of it," or "Take it as a teaching about how to succeed in the future." This kind of advice may help us get back up after being knocked down; it may save us from too much shame and self-hatred; and it may help us reframe our failures in a more positive light.

Some writers and counselors remind us that although we have failed, we have nonetheless survived. Others suggest that we focus on how failure can help build character, courage, and humility. Perhaps most common is the notion that failure can ultimately lead to a more sustainable success via a process of discovering what doesn't work.

This advice can be helpful, but it tends to act more like a salve on our wounds, while supporting the idea that success is what we want and how we handle failure is the matter in question. However, in my practice, I have regularly discovered that *"failure" can serve a deeper psychological function prompting more profound change.* I have found that failure can help us right our ship, align our lives with our values, and walk our own authentic path.

Consider the following alternative views of failure:

Failure as Intelligent Resistance to Our Intended Goal

A client once told me that although she knew she needed to begin an exercise regimen, she kept failing to do so. I asked her, "How come you don't exercise?" She responded, "I just keep blowing it off." Through further inquiry, I discovered that she felt a powerful sense of responsibility to certain people and to accomplishing certain tasks even though she was not fully committed to these people and tasks. She needed to back out of some of these responsibilities but was having a hard time gathering the courage and personal freedom to renegotiate her agreements and relationships.

When I asked her why she didn't make these changes, she said she didn't want to "blow people off." So instead of blowing off other tasks and people, she blew off her commitment to exercise. Her failure had a secret intelligence: she was resistant to being overly responsible and needed to develop, strengthen, and practice this resistance. If we could somehow get her to "succeed" at her exercise goal, we might never discover that she needed to do more than develop physical strength by exercising her body—she needed to build psychological strength by exercising her resistance. It was the power of her resistance, which seemed to be her enemy, that would eventually help her make more radical changes in her relationships and work.

Failure as Course Correction

Failure can also result when the goals we focus on are not our true or deepest goals. People say, "Visualize what you want," "You can't get there if you don't know where you are going," or "Set clear goals and intentions." Here's the trouble with this advice: it assumes that people are conscious of their deepest goals, desires, and intentions. However, if a century of modern Western psychology has taught us one thing, it's that our deepest needs, desires, and nature are mostly unconscious. What happens when we are not conscious of our deeper goals and desires? We often "fail" and seem to be derailed.

This is most evident with addictive patterns, including substance abuse and eating patterns, where the majority of people fail to meet their goals because what they are deeply hungry for is more important than getting clean or thin. I remember a client who had a goal of creating a secure family but kept engaging in risky activities that regularly left him physically hurt (i.e., racing cars and snowmobiles). He wanted me to help him stop these activities so he could be there for his family. The problem was, he loved living on the edge; he needed a way to live there on a more regular basis, or he would fail at building greater security. His deeper goals derailed his less conscious goals.

I have known people who believed they should make more friends, read more, make more time with family, be more politic at work, and increase their earnings so they can buy a fancier car or home. And guess what? If their deeper goals weren't in accord with these goals, they failed to achieve them. In short, failure can be meaningful, turning us away from goals that are less aligned with our deeper selves.

Failure as a Shift in Our Vision of Success

Failure can also result when our very definition of success needs to change, deepen, or conform less to traditional and conventional notions.

Consider the fact that most ideas and images of success are expressed in terms of attainment, increase, growth, or upward movement. We are inundated with ads and other propaganda that focus on obtaining the good life—how to get a better job, a nicer car, healthier relationships, or even more peace. They imply that success means always getting more of something. However, life doesn't necessarily move us upward or in the direction of more; in fact, often our path in life involves dropping down or out, letting go, softening, and nourishing parts of ourselves that don't lead to some kind of linear accumulative development.

This truth was uniquely expressed in a dream I had once. In the dream I was building a business and had an interview with the CEO of American Express, who would be my new client. I was excited as I rode the elevator to the company's penthouse office. After the meeting, I rode down the elevator to the ground floor where two ordinary people were breakdancing. Pointing to the floor, one said, "The vault is down below."

While I was intent on going up, landing the big client, getting on the "American Express train" to success, another part of me was urging me to look downward, dance with regular folks (not the ones who could help my business), and stay closer to the earth than the sky. This dream challenged my definition of success and helped me deepen my values and appreciate qualities that could not be measured or added up. I often find this to be true—that people fail to become "successful" when their notion of success is narrower or more superficial than their dreams or soul long for.

Many believe that we need to get over our fear of failure and aim so resolutely toward success that nothing can stop us. While at times these ideas can serve us, and I have had many successes in my life, it is my failures that have brought me closer to the earth, where I first found love. It is failure that helps me to first hear my own voice, which speaks in response to feeling my shared humanity with others. It is failure that awakens my heart, revealing the steps I must take to follow my own path.

6

Resolutions, Commitments, and All That Jazz: Five Reasons Why Resolutions Fail

Here's my confession: I am a depth psychologist. This means that dreams, the unconscious, the mystery, the unintended—the psyche and soul—are what animate me and inform my perspective. As a depth psychologist, I cringe inwardly every time I see a blog post about New Year's resolutions. While many plainly declare the fact that most resolutions are not kept, their advice about how to improve the percentages is usually superficial.

Here are five mainstream "pearls of wisdom" contrasted with a perspective from depth psychology.

Pearl #1. If you don't make resolutions, you will never get anywhere. In fact, you may be the kind of person who resists making plans and thus has a hard time growing and changing.

Depth Perspective: While much of modern psychology views resistance as a negative thing, I beg to differ. People resist doing what they are "supposed to" for one of two reasons. Either the advice or plan is just not right for the person (regardless of how right it may appear), or the person is tired of accepting the advice and authority of others and is ready to follow their own counsel and wisdom. Thus, if you don't make resolutions or are resistant to planning, look within for your own deeper truths about what is important and how to get there. When this deeper intelligence is supported, you may feel empowered to do what is right for *you*.

Pearl #2. The determining factors for carrying out resolutions are planning, setting reasonable goals, and getting support.

Depth Perspective: People regularly set goals and plans for themselves that are not aligned with their true selves. This happens more than you may think—*we are constantly trying to get ourselves to be some- one that is not exactly who we truly are!* A deeper inquiry via dreams, body, and intuition often reveals that a person's goals are too small, are in need of adjustment, or should be completely abandoned in favor of goals that honor who they really are. For example, a person may want to become slimmer, while their dreams show their need to "take up more space" in the world; or a person may wish to become more disciplined while their psyche calls out for a less linear life.

Pearl #3. Failure is only a temporary setback and great motivator for change.

Depth Perspective: Failure sucks. But it does not indicate a lack of intelligence, motivation, or discipline. It is not necessarily a setback from an effort toward change. Rather, it is information that rises from your deeper self, indicating a need for a shift in perspective, a change in attitude, or a course correction. For example, if you take on a task from a self-critical or self-shaming attitude, you may fail because that background attitude encourages failure. In this way, it is "right" that you fail to follow through with a task you are beating yourself up about.

Pearl #4. Mindfulness can add discipline to your resolutions and render them more restorative and healing.[1]

Depth Perspective: Okay, I know I am stepping on some sacred toes here, but bear with me. Mindfulness can certainly be used to cultivate awareness, but when it is employed as a discipline that overcomes or marginalizes other impulses, as is often the case, then it acts more as a suppressive technique than as a loving one. How can you tell the difference? If mindfulness doesn't work, over and over and over, and you are still using it to assert "your" agenda, *ask yourself, "Is this mindfulness in service of my deepest self or is it in service of an effort to 'fix' myself?"*

Pearl #5. In order to keep your weight-loss resolutions, you must distract yourself from eating.

Depth Perspective: I get it. Many people want to lose weight, eat less, or eat differently. But as I write in the essay "Do You Know Why You Eat? The Key to Losing Weight," people eat beyond their nutritional needs for reasons that they almost never deeply understand. If you think these reasons are to comfort yourself or self-medicate, or because you are lazy or undisciplined, then you too may be guilty of superficial thinking. We eat unhealthily because we are hungry for something deep and true that is largely unknown. If you try to distract yourself from food without exploring what those deeper hungers really are, I suspect (and tons of data confirm) that you will be unsuccessful. And it won't be because you need to improve your skills at distracting yourself!

I have met people who eat to connect with spiritual experiences, to express their power to reach for what they want, to manifest their capacity to say "yes" or "no," or to create stronger boundaries. While you may not agree that these are good reasons to eat, you darn well better discover your own reasons for eating and address them in a more satisfying way before you try to dismiss or override them.

Goals and resolutions can be positive. But be aware that the conscious mind, which is often the author of our goals and plans, is limited. Your soul and psyche may have a more mysterious and magnificent plan for you.

7

To Compromise or Not to Compromise

Many popular psychologists, such as Dr. Phil, preach that compromise is the key to resolving relationship conflict and essential to building sustainable relationships. They view compromise as a "win-win" solution where both parties get some of what they want. However, counselors who hold this perspective tend to act like arbiters, pressing people to compromise regardless of the psychological issues that are fueling their conflicts. When people are unwilling to compromise or don't hold up their end of the agreement, counselors are apt to treat the parties as resistant or unreasonable instead of realizing their approach is inadequate.

For example, imagine that you and I are planning to meet for coffee around noon. You say you'd rather meet at 11:30 a.m.; I respond that 11:30 is a bit early for me, given my schedule, and I'd prefer noon. If neither you nor I have strong feelings or reasons not to compromise, we may decide on 11:45 a.m. Win-win; no problem.

However, when conflicts involve longer-term issues, tensions, or unhealthy patterns of behavior, people tend to be more resistant to making compromises and carrying out agreements. For example, if we are trying to schedule our coffee date, but in the past I have cancelled or shown up late repeatedly, you will be more hesitant to compromise on timing with me. Our history of tension and unresolved conflict makes you appear resistant and unreasonable

because the longer-term pattern has not been addressed. If this issue remains ignored and we are pressured into compromise anyway,
we should expect me to continue the same pattern and/or you to
express your frustration by showing up late or canceling our plans.
The compromise model will be ineffective.

The conflict between Israel and Palestine illustrates the failings
of the compromise model. Diplomats might say, "Can't we get both
sides to make a geographical solution, draw acceptable boundaries,
and create a basic compromise?" When the parties resist, diplomats
will apply pressure to get the parties to compromise. When the
parties continue their resistance or fail to uphold the agreement,
diplomats will blame either the Israelis or Palestinians, but not the
inadequacy of their solution! In this case, both parties have deeper
reasons for not compromising, and what diplomats think is a "win-
win" solution feels more like a "lose-lose" solution to the parties.

I regularly witnessed another example of this phenomenon in
my years of practicing divorce law, when I worked to resolve custody
issues with parents whose longer-term conflicts were never resolved
(that's why they were separating/divorcing). If the court twisted
one parent's arm, saying, "You will deliver that child two days a
week; I don't care whether you like it or not," I came to expect that
parent to get into "traffic delays" or have another excuse for not re-
specting the agreement to deliver the child on time.

Simply put, *the compromise model of conflict resolution rarely
succeeds* when conflict involves a long-term relationship with established patterns of behavior and deeper background tensions.
However, these are exactly the kinds of conflicts that are most important to resolve.

A Psychological Model of Conflict

In my experience as a therapist and attorney, I've found that individuals who resist compromise do not need more pressure to compromise,

but rather more support for their resistance. For example, let's return to the conflict we have about choosing a time to meet for coffee. If you have always been willing to make reasonable compromises but I have regularly failed to show up on time, then you have a good reason to resist the resolution. However, I too may have a good reason to break the resolution. If a counselor were to support your resistance by saying, "I bet you have good reason to not agree to a compromise; please say more about this," you might describe our prior history. And if the counselor said to me, "It appears you are regularly unable to show up at the appointed time; I bet you have good reasons for that as well," I might say, "I have been orienting my schedule every day for the last 10 years around other people and what they want. I'm tired of it!"

Going further to resolve this conflict would mean helping me not agree so readily to meeting at times that don't really work for me and helping you be less agreeable to meeting at times when you doubt I will show up on time. In short, a psychological solution is the exact opposite of the compromise solution. We need support for our resistance to compromise and encouragement to be less agreeable.

Going Deeper: Gender, Sexism, and Compromise

It can be even more difficult to ask people to compromise where long-standing social biases have existed. For example, many counselors suggest that couples need to practice listening more deeply to each other. When one or both parties to the conflict are women, we must consider that as a group, women have long been expected to listen to others and pressured into doing so. Therefore, women may exhibit resistance that is not only directed at their partners but also a response to a history of sacrificing their voices, intelligence, and needs for others. In this case, the psychological model of conflict would suggest furthering women's development by supporting them to speak up more—not to listen more.

This point was brought home to me by a woman who was resistant to listening more to her husband. When I supported her resistance, she said, "I'm tired of listening and sitting there making everyone feel good. Now it's time for me to speak." Supporting her to speak up more is not only good for the longer-term sustainability of her relationship but also for the culture at large, which has marginalized women's intelligence, viewpoints, and voices. Again we see that pressing a person to be more compromising is not always an effective or sustainable solution; instead, a psychological viewpoint is needed. (For more on the impact of sexism on resolving conflict, see the chapter on gender and compromise in my book *Talking Back to Dr. Phil.*)

To be sustainable, resolutions to relationship conflicts need to support people's resistance so that relationships can grow and both people can learn more about themselves and each other. In this way, relationship conflicts are not merely problems to resolve. Like arrows, they point to the next step on the relationship's journey.

8

I'm Sorry:
Three Components of an Effective Apology

Apologizing is often considered an ethical obligation, a responsibility, or simply the right thing to do. But we have gotten so accustomed to hearing, and giving, perfunctory apologies borne out of a sense of obligation that our collective sense of the meaning of an apology has been dulled. For an apology to hold power and value, it must contain three key components:

  1.) A clear statement of the offending action
  2.) An expression of genuine empathy for those aggrieved
  3.) A deep and honest understanding of motivations for the offending action

Without these components, the power of our apologies will decline and their currency will become devalued.

U.S. Senator Mike Crapo's apology for driving under the influence of alcohol is a case in point. On December 23, 2012, Crapo was pulled over by a police officer for running a red light. The officer conducted a field sobriety test, found Crapo to be over the legal blood alcohol limit, and arrested him for driving under the influence.

Crapo's problem was amplified by the fact that he had publically declared himself to be a devout Mormon and as such, never drank alcohol. With all due respect to Senator Crapo (who is simply a straw man for my critique), I will use this case to elucidate the three key components of a potent apology.

Crapo's first apology was issued shortly after the arrest. He said, "I am deeply sorry for the actions that resulted in this circumstance." (In fairness, he said other things as well, but I will focus on this statement for the purposes of this essay.) The vagueness of this apology is telling—it neither mentions what the actions were nor what circumstance resulted from them. He might have said, "I am deeply sorry for drinking after stating that I don't drink, and I'm sorry for getting behind the wheel of a car while intoxicated. These actions have betrayed the trust of those who took me at my word, embarrassed people close to me, and put the lives of others at risk." This would have demonstrated the first two components to a potent apology.

First, it would have demonstrated that he realized what he'd done and had taken responsibility for it. Perhaps the most common and egregious example of neglecting this principle is the statement, "I'm sorry you feel that way," which implies that the offender has not done anything offensive and that any problem is simply in the eye of the offended.

Second, it would have demonstrated empathy for those who had been offended or injured. Crapo's actual statement did not show that he was willing to stand in the shoes of those injured—those put at risk, embarrassed, or betrayed. A common example of this is when people say, "Sorry I'm late," as opposed to "Sorry I kept you waiting, or "Sorry I delayed the meeting," or "Sorry that your time was not valued and respected as it should be." These three statements focus on the offended party rather than the offender. While I realize that this level of apology is not always necessary, the point I am making is that a valuable apology needs to consider the point of view and experience of the person offended.

A potent apology not only takes responsibility for the offensive action but also for what led to that action. Crapo tried to address this issue in his next apology, issued on January 4, 2013, after he pleaded guilty for driving under the influence. In a prepared statement,

Crapo said he had occasionally consumed alcohol during the past months as a way to relieve stress.

The problem here is that Crapo placed the blame and responsibility for his actions on being unable to manage stress. As a culture, we have come to accept the fact that stress is one of the great perpetuators of our problems. We hold it responsible for anger, violence, drinking, addictions, depression, moods, poor health, and more. But is stress really the culprit? I think not. Blaming stress is often an easy way out, one that avoids a deeper psychological explanation and inquiry into our behavior.

I had a client years ago who said he drank because he was stressed. Upon further inquiry, I found out that he did things while drunk that he didn't do while sober, including laughing, singing, and socializing. He didn't really need help to reduce his stress. Resting more and soaking in hot tubs wouldn't have helped him. What he needed was more freedom to have fun, especially with his friends.

Another client told me he drank after work to relieve stress. However, as we discussed this issue, he revealed that drinking helped him communicate more directly with his coworkers and his wife. He didn't use alcohol to reduce his stress; he used alcohol to speak his mind.

Many people use alcohol or other substances to connect with parts of themselves that are marginalized in their daily lives, including feeling ecstasy or other deep emotions, expressing rebellion, being sexual, experiencing religious and spiritual insights, and more. If these deeper motivations and needs are not addressed, "stress" becomes a red herring that simply doesn't have the power to help a person abstain, in a sustainable way, from substances, a fact borne out by the relatively poor success rates of treatment programs.

Whenever I think about apologies, I am reminded of the words of Ntozake Shange in her landmark play, *for colored girls who have considered suicide/when the rainbow is enuf.*

One thing I don't need
   is any more apologies
   i got sorry greetin me at my front door
   you can keep yrs
   [...]
   i cant use another sorry
   next time
   you should admit
   you're mean/low-down/trifling/
   & no count straight out
   steada bein sorry alla the time
   enjoy bein yrself

As Shange suggests, perhaps owning up to who we really are—and learning to enjoy being who we really are—might be less offensive to our senses than an apology that devalues the currency. In other words, perhaps Crapo needs to get to know the part of him that wants to drink and go for a drive instead of just apologizing for it. Maybe then he could live more congruently and be less likely to access this part of himself in a dangerous and deceptive manner.

9

What Is Shame? How Does It Color Our World?

Aparent assaults a child. The other parent looks the other way, rationalizes the assault, minimizes its hurt, or simply doesn't see.[1] What happens to the child psychologically?

The way the event is witnessed by the other parent (or teacher, relative, or community member) will have a longer-term impact even than the assault itself. As this child grows up, they may never talk about the abuse, never seek help, and never take steps to heal for one simple reason: they have internalized the viewpoint of the parent who witnessed the event, and now they too minimize or deny its occurrence.

While the initial assault, like any wound, requires address and redress, the insufficient witnessing wraps the wound in shame. Like a bacteria-laden bandage, it infects the person's beliefs, convincing them that their pain and suffering is the fault of their own inadequacy.

As the child becomes an adult, they may experience a myriad of difficult feelings and patterns of behavior—hurt, fear, insecurity, self-hatred, boundary confusion, difficult relationships, substance abuse, and more. But they may never make a genuine and loving inquiry into the reasons for their suffering. Instead, they conclude that they suffer from certain feelings and patterns of behavior because something is wrong with them, not because something happened to them. In a way, they blame the victim—themselves. Further, they witness their current life from the same internalized viewpoint, rationalizing the disrespect and ill treatment of others, denying their hurts, and feeling a profound sense of wrongness at their core. This is the essence of shame.

People with this history often believe they get hurt because of their own weaknesses rather than because someone has bullied them. They may think they fail because they are stupid or undisciplined rather than because they have unskilled teachers or inadequate support. And they may believe they are treated poorly because they are doing something wrong rather than because their friends, partners, or parents are jealous, moody, or lacking in the capacity to care for another.

I remember a client who had a particularly cold father. Every time she spent time with him, she tried to warm him up by being extra nice and praising him. When his coldness didn't change, she concluded she had failed. It took some time for her to see her father clearly: a man with a coldness that ran through him for reasons entirely independent of her.

I had another client whose husband was particularly frugal despite their relatively comfortable financial status. She would buy shoes and then change the price tags so her husband would not know how much she'd spent. Of course he would see the shoes and inquire about her purchase. After these episodes, she would always feel bad about herself, believing that she either had a spending problem or a dishonesty problem. However, the truth was that he had the spending problem, and her dishonesty sprang from her fear of his reaction. Once she saw this clearly, she was able to be more understanding and compassionate about her circumstances. She stopped feeling ashamed when she purchased shoes and learned ways to be more honest with her husband, not only about her spending but also about her fear of his reactions.

Years ago I had a housemate who often watched TV at night. When I pulled into the driveway, I would see the bluish TV light go out. By the time I opened the door, he would be on the couch reading a book. Why was he hiding his TV watching? It wasn't just that he thought he should be doing more "worthy" activities, but he thought watching TV represented some kind of moral deficiency of his. Because of his shame, it was very difficult for him to inquire about what drew him to watching television. Was it a time of relaxation, was he wanting more "dream time," was he always "on" and wanted to be "off"? As long as he tried to fix his deficiency rather than address his real need and reason for watching TV, he was unlikely to make a change and was highly likely to feel worse about himself.

Shame is called the "master emotion" because so much of our experience is filtered through this lens. It warps and confounds our understanding of ourselves and others in a way that makes finding sustainable resolutions extremely difficult, if not impossible. It leads us to a never-ending cycle of trying to fix ourselves, dismissing our hurts and pains, and essentially living the question: "What's wrong with me?"

10

When "Questions" Shame:
Learning to Be More Direct

P arents ask, "Do you think that was the smart thing to do?" rather than saying, "I don't think that was the smart thing to do." Teachers ask, "Are you sure you want to give that answer?" rather than saying, "That's not the right answer. Try again." Dr. Phil often asks, "What were you thinking?" instead of saying, "I see your actions as hurtful and ill-considered."

Many people, including partners, parents, teachers, and bosses ask questions when they actually want to make a critical or challenging statement. Having practiced law for 10 years, I can attest to the fact that attorneys have made an art of this approach, with questions like, "Didn't you know you were drunk when you got into the car?" and "Did you really think it was okay to threaten someone in order to get your property back?"

Psychologically speaking, when someone asks you this kind of question, they are giving a double message or "double signal" that puts you in a no-win situation: You have been criticized, but you can't respond as such.[1] You are not free to defend yourself or counter the criticism. This approach not only communicates the criticism but also makes you think you shouldn't feel hurt or get defensive. The injury from the criticism is bad enough, but the sense that something is wrong with you for feeling or responding the way you do—that's shame.

Consider the example of Beth and her boss. When Beth proposed a way to streamline her team's weekly meetings, her boss asked, "Do you really think that's a good idea?" While Beth clearly believed her idea was good (or she would not have presented it), she now felt quieted and unsure of how to respond. *What's wrong with my idea—did I present it poorly?* Beth thought. *My boss clearly doesn't like it, but what should I say?* When a colleague asked about the conversation, Beth said, "I always get so insecure when my boss asks me questions. What's wrong with me? I need to be more confident."

The boss's question was a double signal. The surface message asks a simple question requiring a simple answer such as, "Yes, I think it was a good idea." But behind that veil lurks a very different message: "I don't think your idea is a good one," or "I have criticisms of your idea," or even "What are you, some kind of idiot to make such a suggestion?" The "question" is posed as if the boss were open to various responses, but the implied criticism puts Beth on the defensive. It's hard for her to directly respond to this criticism because it is never directly stated.

This puts Beth in a classic double bind: If she responds as if her boss were simply asking a question, nothing she says will satisfy him, because he is *not* asking a question. On the other hand, if Beth responds to the deeper and more potent communication by treating the boss's "question" as if it really is a criticism, he will likely treat her as if she is being inappropriately defensive when, after all, he was "only asking a simple question." This double bind will leave Beth feeling insecure and confused, thinking, "Why can't I get the right answer? What am I missing? Am I some kind of idiot? How embarrassing." She will not only feel that something is wrong with her idea but also that something is wrong with *her* for even suggesting it. In short, she will feel ashamed, a feeling that may become a regular experience around her boss.

The Remedy: Preventing and Healing Shame

If you are the questioner, try turning your question into a statement. Making your criticism clear and direct will give the other person the best chance of responding. Then—and this is very important—let the person know you are open to their agreement or disagreement. For instance, you might say, "Here is my challenge; please feel free to disagree with me." This may lead to a more open debate or conflict, but it will also avoid shaming the other person, thus fostering an empowered, respectful long-term relationship where people feel safe to bring their best insights, feelings, and intelligence forward.

If you are the one questioned, you have two effective options. First, do your best, even after the conversation is over, to see that the question you were asked was not really a question; it was a set-up, a trap. Second, trust that your feelings of frustration and confusion spring from the fact that you were put in a double bind and shamed. Being aware that you have been shamed can help heal the wound on the spot because it stops the internalization, the sense that your feelings have arisen because something is wrong with *you*.

Second, if you become aware of a double signal in the moment, do your best to label what is happening. For example, you might say, "I think you actually have a criticism or challenge for me. Can you please be more direct?" Going further, you might say, "May I respectfully disagree with your criticism?"

If the person gets defensive and refuses to be more direct, you might have to state the criticism and respond to it yourself. This is a rather advanced technique requiring a lot of awareness and detachment in the moment. You might say, "Your question implies a criticism of my idea. You might be thinking (fill in the criticism you suspect the person has). On the other hand, I don't completely agree with that criticism because ..." Essentially, this technique puts you in the driver's seat because you are now modeling the conversation that you and your "criticizer" would have if he or she were more able to engage. Again, this requires a lot of detachment; otherwise, you won't be able to articulate challenges to your own ideas and respond to them.

In summary, criticisms, challenges, and statements that pose as questions are like wolves in sheep's clothing. Not only can they put you in a double bind, but they can also leave you confused, disquieted, and believing that something is wrong with the way you feel. In short, double binds shame. To rectify this situation, you must become aware of this dynamic, see its capacity to cause shame, and make the actual underlying communication as clear and direct as possible.

Good luck!

11

Beyond Individual Psychology: How Psychology Shames

Much of popular psychology presumes that the difficulties a person faces—addiction, depression, anxiety, or low self-esteem—are caused by, and therefore must be addressed by, the individual. This assumption is not always made explicit, but it can be seen in the fact that the counsel provided almost always focuses solely on the individual.

However, we also live in a web of relationships, including family, friendships, organizations, cultures, and subcultures. This web also plays a role in our struggles. For example, it is easy to see that a gay teen's suicidal thoughts stem not only from that person's individual psychology; their suffering is also related to their web of relationships with friends and family, as well as the attitudes and beliefs of the larger culture. The same holds true for people living with addictions and many other psychological difficulties. In the words of Arnold Mindell, Ph.D., these symptoms are "city shadows" —the shadow material of the larger community—which impacts some individuals more than others.[1] Addressing these difficulties must also include making changes in the larger structures of the individual's relationships and viewing the individual in a larger context. Ignoring this context shames the person.

In my experience, there is no symptom that belongs *only* to the individual, whether that symptom is emotional, spiritual, physical, social, or financial. When I work with addicts, I ask myself, "Am I working with one person, or with a family dynamic, a cultural dynamic, or an ethnic dynamic?" When I work with a woman who is suffering from dissatisfaction with her body image or weight, I think, "Am I working with just this woman, or with a gender dynamic, a generational story, or global sexism?" And when I work with a person who has cancer, I question, "Am I working with this one person's health, or with the impact of capitalism's environmental ills, or with a gender issue (e.g., breast cancer, prostate cancer)? And when I work with a person who is depressed, I contemplate, "Is what presses this person down something inside their psyche, or is it a culture that marginalizes their gifts?"

When we don't consider this larger web, we are more likely to feel shame about our suffering and our inability to heal our psychological symptoms. In essence, the individual may believe that their difficulty is *only* about them—their limits, pathologies, deficiencies, failure.

Consider, for example, the fact that many women hate their bodies. Yes, I know "hate" is a strong word, but to call it something else is to underestimate the power of women's internalized criticism. The impact of this self-hatred is evidenced by the voices women have in their heads and the enormous and deadly suffering inherent in eating disorders.

So, when a woman comes to see me, looking to lose weight or change her eating habits, I ask her why she wants to lose weight. When she answers, I listen carefully to hear if she says, "I want to be healthier." If she does say this, it's only part of her dissatisfaction. Usually, she also doesn't like her body and is ashamed of the way it looks.

Why are her emotions so important to account for? Why not just help her change her diet and exercise patterns? The answer is simple: When a woman hates her body, that hatred does motivate her to lose weight, but only in the short term. Over the long term, her psyche almost always fights back, and she gains weight again. In a real way, *she defies the motivation of self-hatred and asserts herself by not following through with her diet.*

Not understanding this gender-related dynamic risks inadvertently adding to the self-hatred and shame that may arise when she believes she has failed.

Or, consider the man who came to me feeling depressed. He complained of "not being able to do anything." When I pressed further, I learned that he was feeling less effective at work and less present for his wife's needs. White and middle class, he had grown up with a father who had driven him to work hard and support his family. Earlier in his life, when his own needs arose, he was able to marginalize them and follow his father's conditioning to focus on work and family. But at the time we met, he could not so easily ignore his deeper needs. The power of those needs now acted like a weight, pulling him down, resisting his old conditioning and tiring him, as if they were trying to get him to drop out of his current life. He experienced this as a kind of depression.

Why not help him with the depression independent of his gender and class? Because understanding him meant understanding the forces that kept him trying to stay "up," trying to be hardworking, productive, and family oriented. If I were to ignore this broader context and simply tell him, "Pay attention to your own needs; stop being there for everyone else!" I would likely fail to lift him from his depression, as my response would not appreciate the power of the pattern established by his father, his father's father, and the patriarchal messages that he had internalized.

These patterns are not benign; they cannot be changed by platitudes like "Just do it." They must be understood for the power they hold over so many men's lives. This person needed to reinvent himself as a man by questioning the values his family and culture supported, and then by finding the courage and fortitude to live differently.

We often seek healing as individuals, and rightly so. But I believe our deeper healing is connected to others—to family, to community, to culture, to the globe. Whether we are gay or straight, white or black, depressed or manic, victim or perpetrator, or rich or poor, the suffering we experience is not only ours. It belongs to us all. We can free each other from the shame of personal failure. When you find it difficult to make certain changes, just know that it may not only be up to you.

12

Winning the Battle with Inner Criticism

"**Y**ou're too fat, too skinny, too sensitive, too insensitive, too talkative, quiet, accommodating, needy, angry, sad, logical, emotional ..." The assault goes on and on. The critical voices in our heads may never stop, may never be satisfied. In fact, most so-called "low self-esteem" is born from incessant inner criticism.

Countering those voices with affirmations like "You're successful and fabulous" may help, but only temporarily. This approach is like telling a bullied child they are beautiful and wonderful, only to send them back to school to be bullied again the next day. A sustainable resolution to bullying requires dealing with the bully; a sustainable resolution to low self-esteem requires dealing with your inner critic.

While our inner criticisms and judgments are often harsh, mean-spirited, and ignorant, that doesn't mean they are not useful to us. They can actually help guide us, but learning how to engage with the different types of self-criticism is key.

What does this intervention look like? Below, I explore three types of critical voices (I call them "inner critics") and ways to lessen the power those voices have over our lives.

Inner Critic as Truth Teller

Not all inner criticism is flat-out wrong; sometimes it contains a grain or two of truth. However, our inner critics are typically not very skillful at delivering this feedback in a way that is helpful and constructive. Critics need to give us specific information with specific suggestions about what to do in order to change. When the criticism just makes us feel bad and offers suggestions that don't work, we need to challenge our inner critics to be more direct, intelligent, caring, and helpful.

For example, if your inner critic says, "You're not keeping up," you might ask probing questions to learn more. "Where am I not keeping up enough? Is it with my ambitions, my self-care, my relationships?"

If your inner critic has given you "advice" in the past that you've never taken, you need to challenge your critic. Ask your critic, "Why do you think your advice never works? Don't just tell me I'm lazy and undisciplined. Alter your advice to help me achieve the change you are suggesting." This is important, because an inner critic can stick to the same old lines for years and years, never considering the possibility that its advice is just not helpful. Unfortunately, many of us are so accustomed to accepting its criticism as truth that we readily believe our critic's explanation of why the advice is not working—an explanation that blames us, not the critic.

When your critic is a truth-teller, you can begin to use this same truth-telling capacity in giving feedback to others. Instead of indulging in generalized judgments of other people, practice giving them direct and useful suggestions that could actually help them improve. Developing this skill is critical in organizations, in schools, in our families, and in our intimate relationships.

Learning to be a truth-teller with others dissipates some of the energy of this kind of inner criticism, lessening the power it has to turn against us.

Inner Critic as Ally to Our Authenticity

Some inner critics jump on us as we begin to express our true selves. They hit us right when and where our spirit or authenticity begins to show. If you are a free spirit, your critic may attack your lack of discipline. If you are non-linear in your approach to life and more focused on the journey than the destination, your critic may attack you for not being more linear and goal-oriented. If you are a feeling-oriented person, your critic may attack you for not being more rational and logical.

You will not silence this kind of critic by resisting it, ignoring it, telling it to shut up, or attempting to think positively. If you try these strategies, the critic will keep re-emerging like Lazarus coming back from the dead, again and again.

To quiet this critic in a more sustainable way, you must come to know and live those aspects of yourself that your critic most fiercely judges. Think of your critic as a person who is really envious of a talent you have and who therefore can't stand it when you start to express that talent.

For example, if you have a particular kind of intelligence, the envious person might say, "Stop trying to be so smart." Or if you are reaching for a goal, they might say, "You'll never make it," or "Your goal is impractical." It's as if the critic were there to point out who you really are.

The great poet, teacher, and author Maya Angelou used this kind of criticism as motivation to write her first book. Her editor told her that writing an autobiography was "almost impossible" and she shouldn't even try it. It turned out that James Baldwin had suggested to her editor that he use reverse psychology, saying, "If you want Maya Angelou to do something, tell her she can't do it."[1]

Inner Critic as Ally to Your Power

Some critics are just against you no matter what you do. They don't have a truth to tell you, and they aren't allies for your authenticity. They just don't like you.

This kind of critic typically doesn't have a theme for its criticism; it just criticizes everything you do. If you eat a bowl of ice cream, it says, "You shouldn't have eaten that ice cream." If you don't eat the ice cream, it says, "Why didn't you go for what you wanted?" If you speak up, it says, "Why did you have to say that?" And if you keep quiet, it says, "Why didn't you speak your mind?" You can't win no matter what you do.

However, this kind of critic does have some important qualities: it is typically fierce, persistent, and strong. It is like the proverbial immovable object that needs to be met by an irresistible force. What is that irresistible force? YOU!

This critic demands that you wrestle with it, fight with it, as a way to gain strength. It is only when your power equals its power—when you realize that its power is *your* power—that you can achieve a sustainable peace.

The bad news is that this task is difficult and probably won't resolve quickly; it can take months or even years. The good news is that in the process of freeing yourself from this kind of criticism, you are becoming a much stronger person who can take on all of life's difficulties with more power, fortitude, resiliency, and commitment.

Inner criticism is epidemic. It is one of the largest but most hidden forms of violence. It can keep us lonely because it causes discomfort when we relate to others. It can keep us from expressing ourselves—our beauty, our intelligence, our gifts. It can drain our joy and confidence. And, make no mistake, it can kill.

To take on such a fierce opponent, we must study it. Simply trying to be positive and kind to ourselves rarely suffices. Get to know your critic, take it seriously, and develop the ability to make sustainable changes in this part of your life. Your efforts will be greatly rewarded.

13

Understanding Dreams About Inner and Outer Criticism

Critics inhabit our outer and inner worlds. Some critics have useful feedback for us, guiding us to hone our skills, open our eyes, and awaken our hearts. However, many critics are neither benign nor beneficial to us. With sharp eyes and red pens, they watch our thoughts, feelings, and actions and invariably conclude that we have erred or are simply unworthy.

In this essay, I unpack three common types of dreams (and their key themes) that highlight the potent dynamics of the critics who bar our path to joy, power, and beauty.

DREAM 1: DEADLY CRITICISM

I dreamed a work colleague told me that she didn't like me, and that nobody else liked me, either. She also told me I wasn't good at working with young people (I am a social worker)—I just thought I was. I was so upset I wanted to kill myself, and I started cutting my wrists! Then I woke up. It was being told I wasn't good at working with young people that really bothered me.

Theme 1: Criticism Can Be Deadly

Being disliked, or being subjected to habitual criticism, can be deadly—literally. We might counter this with, "Don't worry about what others think," or "Don't take it personally." This advice can be helpful, but it also dismisses the impact of such assaults, leaving us feeling ashamed of our vulnerability.

To say it plainly: Being criticized, ostracized, or excluded from our circle of support can kill. Just ask young transgender people, about half of whom "have seriously thought about taking their lives," and one-quarter of whom "report having made a suicide attempt."[1]

Theme 2: Outer Criticism Can Lead to Inner Criticism

This dream is *explicit* about how deadly criticism is for the dreamer: Criticism cuts. Its story suggests that the dreamer cuts herself through criticizing herself or "cutting" herself down.

If you've been the target of intense outer criticism, you may internalize this criticism and use it against yourself, even beneath the level of your own awareness, in a constant self-talk that amounts to death by a thousand cuts. While enduring a mild level of criticism may be bearable, nonstop inner criticism may "add up to a slow and painful demise."[2]

Theme 3: Dreaming of Suicide

We can view the suicide in this dream in two ways. First, as I suggest above, the dreamer is metaphorically killing herself—hurting herself, cutting herself off, or cutting herself down. (I am *not* suggesting that she is *literally* killing herself. That was not the case with this dreamer.)

However, sometimes a dreamer needs to *end* something—kill a pattern, a way of living, or even a belief they have about themselves. It seems this dreamer has internalized the belief that she is not good at what she does. Her dream puts a knife in her hand, suggesting the possibility that she can use this knife to cut herself off from that belief and change her pattern of inner criticism.

Theme 4: The Need for Compassion in Interpreting Dreams

Criticism and unfriendliness is dangerous to this dreamer. This dream highlights our need to be gentle and self-loving when we interpret our dreams. If we are highly self-critical, we may use our dreams as weapons for further self-harm, concluding that our dreams are pointing out ways we are screwing up or failing. This dangerous attitude only feeds into the criticism we are already suffering from.

Directions implied by the dream: If this dream moves you, ask yourself in what ways you cut yourself down or cut yourself off. For example, you might be stifling a creative impulse or holding back from expressing your opinions, your intelligence, your passion. Take your answers to this question seriously. These "cuts" can kill, even if you think you can endure your own silence, your self-abuse, or the abuse of others.

DREAM 2: HERE COMES THE JUDGE

In my dream, I submit a story to be judged, and the judges tell me it is entertaining and full of humor and pathos. But they all keep writing 'D' at the top of the page. So I see all these red 'D's in indelible marker and I can't figure out how to make the story—or my writing in general—better.

Theme 1: The Judge, the Evaluator

Our culture is steeped in the archetype of the judge. Anyone from music teachers and parents to clergy and employers can sit in judgment of your work—and your worth. Of course, we have internalized these behaviors and we judge ourselves, often unfairly.

Theme 2: Submitting to Evaluation

Most of us have little resistance to this kind of judgment because it seems normal and necessary. We have spent many years in school submitting our homework, for example. "It's just the way things are," we might say, or "I need to get feedback and evaluation to improve and grow." In short, we *submit*, as does the dreamer who "submits" her story, without critical reflection about the fairness or intent of the judge.

The definition of the word "submit" is instructive here: "to accept or yield to a superior force or to the authority or will of another person."

Whether evaluation comes from inside or outside ourselves, we accept the judge's ruling or grade as if it were accurate, as if it were *truth*. With little critical evaluation of the judge or judgment, we begin working to change ourselves, ignoring the injury to our self-esteem. In the language of the dream, these judges can leave an indelible mark on us—a lasting opinion of our own value—as they have on the dreamer's evaluation of her writing.

This kind of judgment is epidemic when it comes to weight loss and body image, especially for women who judge themselves every day when looking in the mirror or stepping on the scale. Many submit too readily to this judgment and rush into weight-loss programs, even though they rarely work. This kind of judgment leaves an indelible mark on these individuals' sense of beauty and worth.

Directions implied by the dream: One way to work with the judgment dynamic is to integrate the power of the judge. Some benefit by judging the judge, asking, "Who are *you* to judge me? Are you fair? Do you always criticize and never praise? Do you empower me to make sustainable changes, or do you just leave me feeling worse about myself?" In asking these questions, we can take the judge's power and use it to think critically about judgments we receive.

DREAM 3: HIDING FROM THE CRITIC

I dreamed I was at work, filling out a FedEx form so I could send my résumé to a potential employer, when my boss came near. I tried to hide the form from her so she wouldn't know I was planning to leave for a better job. Just then I looked up and saw a group of redcoats coming toward me, brandishing rifles with bayonets. I panicked and ran the other way, down the hill into the woods. I woke up in a state of anxiety.

Theme 1: Keeping Ourselves in the Dark

This dreamer wants to make a change in her life. However, a boss (a person with power or authority over the dreamer) is actively working against her change. Real people in the dreamer's life, as well as the dreamer herself, are likely to hold this antagonistic viewpoint. The dreamer handles this antagonism by trying to hide her true intention to make a life change.

This kind of hiding is actually quite common: Many of us don't tell others, or ourselves, what we really want. For example, I left my consulting firm in 1994. About a year before that, I started showing up late, missing deadlines, taking longer lunches, and working below my potential. My behavior showed that I wanted a change—but I couldn't face the implications of actually leaving, as it would threaten my financial security and cause conflict in my relationships. Eventually, I heard myself say to a friend, "I don't want to do this kind of work any more. I want to study clinical psychology." I wasn't ready until that moment; I couldn't deal with the revolution—changing my home, significant relationships, and source of income.

Theme 2: Starting a Revolution

The dreamer tries to hide her intentions, but apparently she cannot. She must face her resistance to making a change. In real life, she hadn't fully owned and declared her intention to leave her job.

Facing the resistance means engaging in a kind of revolution, a war. The dreamer must deal with the counter-revolutionary forces —the redcoats. Apparently, her secret is not so safe, or these counter-revolutionary forces would not be so clearly represented in the dream. She doesn't feel ready to fight, but the battle is on. She is in a state of conflict and anxiety.

In real life, this dreamer was worrying about her financial security and about letting others down. The dream suggested that she needed to face her fears and fight for her independence. (This dreamer did just that: She changed her job and her entire lifestyle.)

Directions implied by the dream: If this dream resonates for you, you may ask yourself how or what you are hiding. Are you aware of your deepest intentions, hopes, and dreams? Whom do you keep them hidden from? Often our inner and outer critics have never lived their dreams, and they may be envious of anyone's movement toward freedom, self-love, and the expression of their true gifts and passions.

14

Getting Real:
Seven Roadblocks to Becoming
Our Authentic Selves

Get real, be authentic, be yourself. It's good advice. But what makes being who we truly are so damn difficult? What are the roadblocks that hinder the project of being and becoming ourselves? Here are seven problems many face:

#1: The Problem of Abuse and Trauma

How many of us have suffered some level of trauma or abuse, whether at home, at school, among friends, or in the public sphere? I daresay that almost all of us have some scars and defense mechanisms designed to help us cope and survive. In fact, some of these coping mechanisms survive for years or generations after the traumatic event, especially for victims of child abuse, sexual abuse, racism, and other egregious harm. This fact led famed psychoanalyst Donald Winnicott to the notion of a "false self"—a persona or "defensive façade"—that many of us develop early in life as a protection from re-experiencing trauma.[1] The problem is that the "true self"—the one based on authentic experience—is hidden, suppressed, and often unknown. "If you are bold enough to confront, take on, or critique a false-self behavior … well … look out," writes psychologist Dr. Tian Dayton.[2]

Getting real is no easy task; those who were comfortable with your former façade may meet your efforts with resistance and hostility.

#2: The Problem of Restrictive Gender Roles

Cultural norms and powerful stereotypes abound about how men and women *should* feel and behave. In fact, one of the best-selling books of all time, perhaps outsold only by *The Bible* and Mao's *Little Red Book*, is John Gray's *Men Are from Mars, Women Are from Venus,* which has sold over 50 million copies![3]

If we believe Gray, men are thinkers, while women are feelers; men strive to solve problems, while women complain so they will be listened to; men deal with stress through solitude, while women deal with stress through talking; men are happy when they accomplish goals, while women are happy when they feel nurtured.[4] Much of mainstream culture views these differences between men and women as predictable and invariable. But modern wisdom, research, and experience clearly show that these phenomena are more accurately seen as social scripts dictating how we are supposed to act, not as how we truly are.[5] Says Drs. Nelwyn B. Moore and J. Kenneth Davidson Sr., "Although there are some genetically determined sex differences, most are not innate but instead have been learned through socialization."[6]

Men's true selves suffer when they are encouraged, even psychologically coerced, into being stoic, aggressive, and essentially anti-feminine.[7] A telltale symptom of this bias is the fact that over 20 million men have used Viagra, and many are becoming dependent on it. College students are even taking Viagra at parties just for fun.[8] On the other hand, most men won't seek counseling even though 6 million men suffer from depression![9] Men are "trying to be men"—meaning being hard and ready as opposed to being vulnerable and emotive or asking for help.

The roles of women in society are arguably even more restrictive. Sexist stereotypes are promulgated even by the likes of Harvard President Lawrence Summers, who argued that men outperform women in math and sciences because of biological difference. Summers also conveniently ignored the realities of sexism when he stated that discrimination is no longer a career barrier for female academics.[10]

And most recently, Microsoft CEO Satya Nadella told an audience full of women in technology that they shouldn't ask for raises, implying that silence is the key to their success in the workplace.[11] Apparently, being an empowered woman valued for her intelligence, creativity, and wisdom is still met with ignorance and mean-spiritedness from leaders of our most influential universities and corporations.

The pressure to conform to gender roles impacts women and men psychologically, emotionally, physically, and financially, keeping people from expanding their identities beyond the limits of traditional roles.

#3: The Problem of Trying to Look Good
(including appearing healthy, fit, confident, happy, and spiritual)

In case you haven't noticed, the way we are supposed to look, behave, and feel is clearly defined by mainstream culture. The evidence is everywhere: a $60-billion diet industry; magazine covers showing idealized bodies. And let's not forget the ubiquitous articles and blog posts telling us how to appear confident (regardless of how sensitive we are), how to look younger (regardless of how mature we are), and how to avoid looking nervous (regardless of the situation). On the spiritual front, we are told to be grateful and forgiving; on the physical front, we are told what to eat and how to sleep; on the relational front, we are told how to communicate, make love, and choose partners. You have a veritable set of instructions on "how to be you," except that it excludes the most important component —who you really are!

Personally, I try to take the advice Maya Angelou offers in her poem "On the Pulse of Morning" about how to take what is deepest and truest inside of us and make it visible to the world. "Mold it into the shape of your most/Private need. Sculpt it into/The image of your most public self."[12]

#4: The Problem of Conventional Notions of Success

Our paths are as varied as we are diverse. Some people serve, some pursue money, some take care of children, some make art, some wash dishes, some are too disabled physically or emotionally to work in the world, and some turn their energies toward pursuits that are not conventionally valued. Nonetheless, there is a great societal pressure to gain status and income (besides a real need to have a life-sustaining level of income).

I have no quarrel with status or financial success. But I'm aware that when these become the basis of our self-evaluation, we begin to curb and cut off aspects of ourselves that don't fit. Qualities that do not resonate with market values, like tenderness or sensitivity, do not flourish. We may reject life paths that foster less conventional forms of success. As opposed to popular slogans such as, "Do what you love and the money will follow," I would rather promote the wisdom, "Do what you want and you get the satisfaction of doing what you want." Whether money and traditional success will follow is not a certain thing.

Noted intellectual Dr. Cornel West writes, "When you end up obsessed with success rather than greatness, prosperity rather than magnanimity, security rather than integrity—you end up with a generation of peacocks." The problem is, "peacocks strut because they can't fly."[13]

Also, this kind of peacock cannot express our individuality.

#5: The Problem of Being Rational at the Expense of Our Feelings

Mainstream thinking promotes the belief that our emotions get in the way of our ability to be rational. This model of valuing rationality and alienating our emotions has dominated our thinking.[14]

Our feelings, however, have an intelligence of their own. We feel hurt because something is hurting us; we feel angry because something is provoking our reaction; we feel compassion because we are moved to empathize. Even uncomfortable feelings like depression, sadness, and anxiety are worthy of our understanding because they offer insight into who we are and the conditions we find ourselves in. In fact, of all today's problems and conflicts, it is emotional difficulties that require the most attention and understanding. Our insistence that we must resolve problems by being more rational acts as a fierce form of denial.

The continual encouragement to be rational at the expense of our feelings is dangerous to the project of being and becoming our authentic selves as well as to building relationships with the earth, its creatures, and the rest of the human family.

#6: The Problem of Perfectionism

Seeking the right answer and trying to be perfect can turn us away from following our deeper instincts and truths. In the words of psychologist Gordon Flett, Ph.D., who spent decades researching perfectionism, "For many perfectionists, that 'together' image is just an emotionally draining mask and underneath they feel like imposters." Perfectionism derails our progress toward becoming ourselves.

Alarmingly, Dr. Flett found that perfectionism can actually be deadly and that many people who commit suicide are afraid of failure, the other side of perfectionism.[15]

#7: The Problem of Fundamentalism

Holding onto absolutes, especially in terms of right and wrong, often devolves into fundamentalist beliefs that injure the self and others through stereotypes and projection.

Fundamentalism is marked by a deeply held set of beliefs that identify one set of teachings as the fundamental truth, which is diametrically opposed to a conflicting idea that is fought against. "It provides a sense of security when the sense of self is shaky," and "Reality is replaced with delusions, perspectives with myopia."[16]

Fundamentalism is not limited to the domain of religion. Some are fundamentalists about money, measuring the value of everything in financial terms because they believe that money is the ultimate measure of worth. Some are fundamentalists regarding personal independence and other life philosophies. And many are fundamentalists about their perspective on reality, lecturing their friends, family members, and others about which points of view are "just not reality" or "not the way things really are."[17]

These rigidly held beliefs close the mind and heart to the myriad paths and possibilities of expression that we are capable of, the expressions inherent to our natures. They create a fiercely defended opposition to any movement outside these beliefs, even when that movement indicates who we really are.

Carl Jung held that individuation—the process of unfolding the flower that we are into an expression of our deepest and truest selves—is the essential goal of psychology. This task is met with dragons, demons, and giants as well as guardian angels and helping hands. The rewards can only be assessed by the resonant sound our soul makes when we listen deep inside. The costs of abandoning the project can be witnessed in the downcast faces of the soulless and depressed. We can fight the dragons, even slay them at times; we can follow our nighttime and daytime dreams; we can find allies to cry out with us; we can meet the challenge of our life project with a clear and certain *"yes."* That is my hope; that is my intention in beginning to identify the roadblocks along the way.

15

The Courage to Find Soul: A Call for More "Psyche" in Psychology

The word "psyche" is synonymous with "soul"; accordingly, psychology could be considered as the art and science of healing and nourishing the soul. But what if healing and nourishing our souls means taking a path that is less pretty than we want? What if the soul were like an inner activist—disrupting our status quo, creating imbalance, finding nourishment in illness, moving us not only into the light but also into the shadow, and rendering us unsure of even our most cherished beliefs? Would you still follow her?

Consider the following cases:

Case 1:

Brad, a multi-millionaire, retired in his early fifties. He worried about money all the time. He was almost obsessed with counting it and reviewing his budget; he was afraid to spend too much, limiting himself to spending only a portion of the interest he made each month while his net worth grew. Therapists and friends told him to spend more, worry less, buy the luxury car he eyed, go on the vacations he fantasized about, and send his lower-income friends plane tickets to visit him. But he couldn't.

"Maybe I'll never get over this worry," Brad said. "Maybe it's the legacy of my father, who was incredibly frugal and anxious about money." Instead of trying to relieve him of his worry, I assumed that his worry took him in a meaningful direction regarding money and more. I asked him to tell me what it was like to worry about money. He became vulnerable, sensitive, even fragile. As he spoke, I noticed that our level of emotional intimacy was deepening, and our conversation meandered into new territory, including his deep love for animals and his desire to help build homes for people who couldn't afford them. His worry about money was a doorway to his more tender feelings and care for others—his connection with humanity. His worry was an invitation, a teaching, not an illness to be relieved.

Case 2:

Sue regularly fought with her father. Just thinking of him made her angry. She tried meditating to let go of her anger, but it always returned. I asked Sue to show me the anger with her hand. She made a fist and stuck out her jaw. I asked this angry part of her, "What kind of person are you?" She replied, "I do what I want, go for what I want. I don't take sh-t from anyone."

As she learned to take less sh-t in many areas of her life, not just with her father, her resentment toward her father began to fade. Her anger gave her access to her power, a power that was meant to be used, not meditated away.

Case 3:

Sally suffered bouts of depression and was afraid to get pulled down again. She had been there before, and it wasn't pretty. I said, "Let's go down together. Let me be your eyes and ears and see what we can find."

We sunk together, first into a low mood, then into tears and sadness. I asked, "Dear sadness, why have you come?" She replied, "I miss the hopes and dreams I had when I was a child; somehow they got lost along the way." Thank goodness for her depressed state. Without it she would never have remembered the life that she really wanted.

We naturally seek to rid ourselves of anything that seems to interfere with our goals and sense of wellness. We fight against depression—we "anti depress." We meditate hoping to make our anger go away and practice mindfulness to stop ourselves from being so damn hungry. We learn communication skills in order to listen better, speak more directly, and avoid hurtful conflicts. We try to muster sufficient resolve to free ourselves from bad habits and addictions.

As men, we treat our softness, especially if it shows up in our penises, as something to be ashamed of and corrected (making Viagra one of the best-selling drugs on the planet). As women, we obsess about our body shapes and sizes (making the diet industry a $60-billion gold mine).[1] We see everything that disturbs us as an enemy to overcome or a disease to be conquered, treated, fixed, and made to go away.

But what if treating and overcoming our symptoms takes us away from our deeper healing? What if those things that disturb us the most are keys to our authentic selves? What if the medicine we really long for can be found cooking, alchemically, right in the center of what we think of as illness? What if bringing an attitude of love and awareness to our problems instead of treating and fixing them is what really nourishes our souls? Would you take that path? Would you follow your soul?

16

Death, Dying, and Altered States: Bridging Two Realities

visited my mother just a few months before she passed in 2011. We dined in a restaurant attached to a casino. After dinner she went to play blackjack and I went to the bathroom. I came back minutes later, took a seat next to her, and asked, "How's it going?"

She looked at me strangely, clutched her purse, and said, "I'm waiting for my son."

I replied, "I'm sure he'll be back soon."

In her final months, my mother was often in an altered state —a way of perceiving and communicating that was outside of conventional reality. We went on imagined vacations and cruises together; we recreated history (stories that strayed from truth but that we nonetheless "agreed" were truth). I even gave her a new Spanish name that made her giggle and helped me let go of the person she used to be. I saw no reason to insist on conventional reality or my reality. In fact, her altered state allowed us to begin a new chapter in our relationship, one I am very thankful for.

Joining her reality allowed a sweet healing. As a youth, I was the black sheep of the family. I was challenging in my viewpoints and underappreciated for my perspective. However, being an outsider left me longing for her understanding—an understanding I had long since let go of ever getting. A few weeks before she died, she looked at me with love and appreciation and said, "How did you get this way? You're such a deep and caring man." It touched my heart deeply to know she would never have seen me this way or uttered those words when she was in her "right mind."

Recently, I shared this story online with friends, who responded with their own stories. One friend was amazed at the relationship she had developed with her father just before he died and the things she had learned from him. She wrote, "I met monkeys in the kitchen with my father, took walks to radiography labs down the street, and learned about his childhood in stories he had never shared before." She continued, "Journey with your elders, friends; they are no longer what you think they are supposed to be, but who they become can be amazing."

Another friend, Tamara, also explored letting go of her reality and opening to her mother's altered state. She wrote, "My mom has created some cool new stories in recent years, including that she visited the North Pole and that she used to surf! I think it is a little harder for me to drop the part that wants to correct the story when the person is still mostly in a familiar state than when the person is more often in other states. I am finding it easier to flow with my mom now that she is more often in other states."

And then there is Rich, who felt misunderstood by his mother most of his life. He thought her altered state would allow her the opportunity to see him differently. While this did not happen, her new reality was nonetheless freeing. He said, "During the advanced stages of her Alzheimer's, my mother became fun-loving and animated ... much unlike the mother I knew. I will always remember one of our last meetings, during which I (ill advisedly!) attempted to come up with a very sincere, heartfelt "capstone" statement laying out who I felt I had become and what my priorities are in life. She listened with a curious intensity and attention. When I was done, she looked into my eyes and said, 'You gotta mend your ways!' I almost fainted. The stunning part for me was that in her state, she had expressed the fractal, the essence of the pattern, that had defined our relationship for our entire history!"

Kelley found herself able to let go of conventional reality and just enjoy a woman she cared for in a nursing home. She wrote, "I repeatedly celebrated an elderly woman's sweet 16th birthday in a nursing home; it was a blast for both of us every time."

Neal was touched by the final moments he spent with his grandfather. While his grandfather had some capacity to communicate normally, he shared a dream (a kind of altered reality) that was particularly meaningful. Neal wrote, "I got to visit my grandfather in the hospital the day before he passed away. I came in from college to see him. My mom told me that he was no longer conscious, but when I walked into the room, he was fully awake and we had a great conversation for a couple of hours. He told me he dreamed that he and I were fishing on my boat (we went fishing a lot together) and it seemed so real. He passed away the next day. It is one of the most powerful memories I have and one I will never forget."

Another friend, Steven, was struck by his father's unintended, yet marvelous, sense of humor. Rather than trying to help his father understand, he simply enjoyed him. He reported, "My dad had an aide, Gene. But he calls him Sidney, and now so does everyone else when they're around my dad. One day Gene walked out of the room, and Dad asked where he was. He was told Sidney would be back in a few minutes. Dad said, 'Oh, he's back from Australia?'"

And finally, Edie wrote, "End-of-life times can be incredibly precious; I had that with my mother as well. We went on 'trips' too. My favorite was Hawaii, where neither of us had gone in this lifetime."

I readily understand the grief and heartache that sometimes arises when a loved one is no longer "here" communicating in conventional reality. I understand the impulse to correct them and somehow bring them back to a world in which we are familiar. But consider the possibility of entering the world of your loved one, their altered state. If you can, enjoy it. You may discover a relationship that has always been there waiting for you—one you may not want to miss.

Notes

Introduction

1) Heidi Blake, "Why Women Think They Are Fat: Brain 'Thinks Body Is Two Thirds Bigger Than It Is,'" *The Telegraph,* posted June 15, 2010, accessed on March 21, 2016, http://www.telegraph.co.uk/news/health/news/7826822/Why-women-think-they-are-fat-brain-thinks-body-is-two-thirds-bigger-than-it-is.html.

2) Arnold Mindell, *City Shadows: Psychological Interventions in Psychiatry* (Portland, OR: Lao Tse Press, 2009).

3) "Cheating Is a Personal Foul," *The Educational Testing Service / Ad Council Campaign to Discourage Academic Cheating,* 1999, accessed March 15, 2015, http://www.glass-castle.com/clients/www-nocheating-org/adcouncil/research/cheatingfactsheet.html.

4) Max and Ellen Schupbach, "Our Logo," *Deep Democracy Institute,* accessed March 21, 2016, http://www.deepdemocracyinstitute.org/en/our-credo-our-logo/eventmont/2016/10.html.

5) Michael Ventura, "Letters at 3am: James Hillman (1926-2011): Remembering James Hillman," *AustinChronicle.com,* posted January 13, 2012, accessed March 21, 2016, http://www.austinchronicle.com/columns/2012-01-13/letters-at-3am-james-hillman-1926-2011/.

6) "Freud's Seduction Theory," *Wikipedia*, accessed March 21, 2016, https://en.wikipedia.org/wiki/Freud%27s_seduction_theory.

7) Gregory M. Herek, "Facts About Homosexuality and Mental Health," *Sexual Orientation: Science, Education, and Policy,* accessed March 21, 2016, http://psc.dss.ucdavis.edu/rainbow/HTML/facts_mental_health. html.

8) Alan Schwarz and Sarah Cohen, "A.D.H.D. Seen in 11% of U.S. Children as Diagnoses Rise," *NYTimes.com*, posted March 31, 2013, accessed March 21, 2016, http://www.nytimes.com/2013/04/01/health/more-diagnoses-of-hyperactivity-causing-concern.html?pagewanted=all.

9) Ibid.

10) Garth Kant, "Radical Increase in Kids Prescribed Ritalin," *WND,* posted April 1, 2013, accessed March 21, 2016, http://www.wnd.com/2013/04/radical-increase-in-kids-prescribed-ritalin/.

11) Mandy Silver, "Cornel West Delivers 'Inspiring' Lecture," *Student Life*, posted February 3, 2006, accessed March 21, 2016, http://www.studlife.com/archives/News/2006/02/03/CornelWestdeliversinspiringlecture/.

12) In conversation with Jewish psychologists Dawn Menken, Ph.D., author of *Raising Parents, Raising Kids: Hands-on Wisdom for the Next Generation*, and Gary Reiss, Ph.D., author of *Beyond War and Peace in the Arab Israeli Conflict.*

13) Karina L. Walters and Jane M. Simoni, "Reconceptualizing Native Women's Health: An "Indigenist" Stress-Coping Model," *American Journal of Public Health*, 92, no. 4 (2002): 520-524.

14) Ibid.

15) Brooke Axtell, "How to Be a Shameless Woman: Making Peace with Our Bodies, Ourselves," *Forbes.com*, posted September 26, 2012, accessed March 23, 2016, http://www.forbes.com/sites/shenegotiates/2012/09/26/how-to-be-a-shameless-woman-making-peace-with-our-bodies-ourselves/.

16) Shari Roan, "Keeping It Off," *LATimes.com*, posted June 2, 2008, March 21, 2016, http://articles.latimes.com/2008/jun/02/health/he-regain2.

17) James Baldwin, *The Fire Next Time* (New York: The Dial Press, 1963), 19-20.

18) Excerpt from Julie Diamond, Ph.D.'s endorsement of my book *Talking Back to Dr. Phil: Alternatives to Mainstream Psychology* (Santa Fe: Belly Song Press, 2013).

S e c t i o n I
Racism, Anti-Semitism, and Homophobia: Witnessing Social Justice

1. The American Soul: Honoring Our Black Elders

1) Cornel West, *Never Forget: A Journey of Revelations* (Los Angeles: Hidden Beach Records, 2007), compact disc.

2) James Melvin Washington, ed., "A Slave Woman's Prayer (1816)," found by Stephen Hays, *Conversations with God: Two Centuries of Prayers by African Americans* (New York: HarperPerennial, 1994): 19.

3) Rainer Maria Rilke, *The Book of Hours*, trans. Robert Bly, posted by *Nebraska Zen Center Heartland Temple*, accessed March 28, 2016, http://www.prairiewindzen.org/zen_european_poetry.html.

4) "Du Bois and the Question of the Color Line: Race and Class in the Age of Globalization," *Journal of the Research Group on Socialism and Democracy Online*, posted April 19, 2011, accessed March 28, 2016, http://sdonline.org/33/du-bois-and-the-question-of-the-color-line-race-and-class-in-the-age-of-globalization/.

5) James Baldwin, *The Fire Next Time* (New York: The Dial Press, 1963), 23.

2. MLK Today: Taking the Blinders off White Privilege

1) Ronald Turner, "Misusing MLK Legacy and the Colorblind Theory – II. Martin Luther King, Jr.'s Color-Awareness," *Race, Racism and the Law*, accessed March 28, 2016, http://www.racism.org/index.php?option=com_content&view=article&id=869:justice06-1&catid=143&Itemid=120&showall=&limitstart=2.

2) Beverly Daniel Tatum, *Why Are All the Black Kids Sitting Together in the Cafeteria? And Other Conversations About Race* (New York: Basic Books, 2003), 20–21.

3) Terry Levine, "Sincere Ignorance and Conscientious Stupidity," *Terry Levine* (blog), posted July 11, 2011, accessed March 28, 2016, http://www. terrylevine.com/2011/07/sincere-ignorance-and-conscientious-stupidity.html.

4) "The Slow and Tortured Death of Affirmative Action," *The Black Commentator* (blog), accessed March 28, 2016, http://www.blackcommentator .com/49/49_cover.html.

5) Jeff Wattrick, "Yes, Henry Payne, Martin Luther King Really Did Support Affirmative Action," *Deadline Detroit*, posted August 28, 2013, accessed March 28, 2016, http://www.deadlinedetroit.com/ articles/6195/yes_henry_payne_martin_luther_king_really_did_ support_affirmative_action#.VLV_cUvOXKA.

6) Marianne Bertrand, "Racial Bias in Hiring: Are Emily and Brendan More Employable than Lakisha and Jamal," *The University of Chicago Graduate School of Business*, 4, no. 4 (2003), accessed March 28, 2016, http://www.chicagobooth.edu/capideas/spring03/racialbias.html.

7) "Stop-and-Frisk Data," *New York Civil Liberties Union*, accessed March 28, 2016, http://www.nyclu.org/content/stop-and-frisk-data.

8) Katherine Beckett and Heather Evans, "The Role of Race in Washington State Capital Sentencing 1981-2012," *Death Penalty Information Center*, posted January 27, 2014, accessed March 28, 2016, http:// www.deathpenaltyinfo.org/documents/WashRaceStudy2014.pdf.

9) Langston Hughes, "Justice," *Poem Hunter*, accessed March 28, 2016, http://www.poemhunter.com/poem/justice/.

3. Dreaming King's Dream Forward: Reflections on America's Psyche

1) David Van Biema, "Mother Teresa's Crisis of Faith," *Time.com*, posted August 23, 2007, accessed March 17, 2015, http://content.time.com/ time/magazine/article/0,9171,1655720,00.html.

2) June Jordan, *Technical Difficulties* (North Pomfret, VT: Trafalgar Square Books, 1993), 106.

3) Ibid, 117.

4) Address to civil rights marchers by the Rev. Dr. Martin Luther King Jr. in Washington, D.C. on August 28, 1963. "Full Text of King's 'I Have a Dream' Speech," *ChicagoTribune.com*, posted January 31, 2013, accessed March 17, 2015, http://www.chicagotribune.com/news/nationworld/sns-mlk-ihaveadream-story.html#page=1.

5) Dr. King first delivered this sermon at Ebenezer Baptist Church, where he served as co-pastor. On Christmas Eve, 1967, the Canadian Broadcasting Corporation aired this sermon as part of the seventh annual Massey Lectures. Martin Luther King, Jr., "A Christmas Sermon on Peace, 1967," accessed January 14, 2013, http://www.ecoflourish.com/Primers/education/Christmas_Sermon.html.

6) Robert S. Boynton, "Detour to the Promised Land," *NYTimes.com*, posted January 23, 2000, accessed March 17, 2015, http://www.nytimes.com /books/00/01/23/reviews/000123.23boynt.html.

7) Martin Luther King, Jr., *Strength to Love* (Philadelphia: Fortress Press, 1963), 13.

8) "Martin Luther King, Jr.," *America's Story from America's Library*, accessed March 17, 2015, http://www.americaslibrary.gov/aa/king/aa_king_subj.html.

9) Gita Brown, "Segregation is Back in America's Public School," *Rhode Island College*, posted November 2, 2009, accessed March 17, 2015, http://www.ric.edu/news/details.php?News_ID=652.

10) Cornel West, *Hope on a Tightrope* (New York: Smiley Books, 2008), 38.

11) Frances Rice, "Why Dr. Martin Luther King, Jr. Was a Republican," *National Black Republican Association Newsletter*, accessed January 13, 2013, http://suwanneegop.com/NBRA%20Civil%20Rights%20Newsletter-2.pdf.

12) Daniel Denvir, "Meet MLK's Glenn Beck-Loving Niece," *Salon*, posted August 27, 2010, accessed January 13, 2013, http://www.salon.com/2010/08/27/alveda_king_glenn_beck/.

13) "Full Text of King's 'I Have a Dream' Speech."

14) Jared Taylor, *Paved With Good Intentions: The Failure of Race Relations in Contemporary America* (New York: Carroll & Graf Publishers, 1993).

15) Jerome McCristal Culp, Jr., "Colorblind Remedies and the Intersectionality of Oppression: Policy Arguments Masquerading as Moral Claims," *New York University Law Review,* 69 no. 163 (1994): 164-165.

4. What's the Matter with "All Lives Matter"?

1) *Black Lives Matter* (website), accessed August 15, 2015, http://blacklives matter.com.

2) "Stop-and-Frisk Data," *New York Civil Liberties Union*, accessed August 15, 2015, http://www.nyclu.org/content/stop-and-frisk-data.

3) *Death Penalty Information Center* (website), accessed August 15, 2015, http://www.deathpenaltyinfo.org/race-and-death-penalty.

4) Marianne Bertrand, "Racial Bias in Hiring: Are Emily and Brendan More Employable than Lakisha and Jamal," *The University of Chicago Graduate School of Business*, 4, no. 4 (2003), accessed August 15, 2015, http://www.chicagobooth.edu/capideas/spring03/racialbias.html.

5) "Discount Babies," *Economist.com*, posted May 14, 2010, accessed August 15, 2015, http://www.economist.com/blogs/freeexchange/2010/05/markets_everything.

6) "Interview with Beverly Daniel Tatum," *PBS.com*, posted 2003, accessed August 15, 2015, http://www.pbs.org/race/000_About/002_04-background-03-04.htm.

7) Beverly Daniel Tatum, *Why Are All the Black Kids Sitting Together in the Cafeteria? And Other Conversations About Race* (New York: Basic Books, 2003).

8) Jarune Uwujaren, "If You 'Don't See Race,' You're Not Paying Attention," *Everyday Feminism*, posted September 11, 2013, accessed August 15, 2015, http://everydayfeminism.com/2013/09/dont-see-race/.

9) "Satchel," (video) *Black Lives Matter*, accessed August 15, 2015, http://blacklivesmatter.com/i-imagine-visions/satchel/ (page since deleted).

5. America's Deadly Denial of Racism

1) "Shooting of Walter Scott," *Wikipedia*, accessed February 2, 2016, https://en.wikipedia.org/wiki/Shooting_of_Walter_Scott.

2) Andy Campbell, "Florida Cops Fired over Racist Texts, KKK Video," *The Huffington Post*, posted March 22, 2015, accessed February 2, 2016, http://www.huffingtonpost.com/2015/03/22/cops-fired-racist-video _n_6918652.html?fb_action_ids=824529154261943&fb_action_ types=og.comments.

3) Jamelle Bouie, "The Gulf that Divides Us," *Slate*, posted October 17, 2014, accessed February 2, 2016, http://www.slate.com/articles/news _and_politics/politics/2014/10/the_whiteness_project_whites_ and_blacks_are_still_living_in_separate_worlds.html.

4) Ana Swanson, "Whites Greatly Overestimate the Share of Crimes Committed by Black People," *WashingtonPost.com*, posted December 1, 2014, accessed February 2, 2016, http://www.washingtonpost.com/ blogs/wonkblog/wp/2014/12/01/whites-greatly-overestimate-the-share-of-crimes-committed-by-black-people/.

5) Max Ehrenfreund, "17 Disturbing Statistics from the Federal Report on Ferguson Police," *WashingtonPost.com*, posted March 4, 2015, accessed February 2, 2016, http://www.washingtonpost.com/blogs/ wonkblog/wp/2015/03/04/17-disturbing-statistics-from-the-federal-report-on-ferguson-police/.

6) Marianne Bertrand, "Racial Bias in Hiring: Are Emily and Brendan More Employable than Lakisha and Jamal," *The University of Chicago Graduate School of Business*, 4, no. 4 (2003), accessed February 2, 2016, http://www.chicagobooth.edu/capideas/spring03/racialbias.html.

7. The Holocaust and the Inner Ghetto: The Psychology of Jewish Suffering

1) Eric Lichtblau, "The Holocaust Just Got More Shocking," *NYTimes. com*, posted March 1, 2013, accessed March 28, 2016, http://www. nytimes.com/2013/03/03/sunday-review/the-holocaust-just-got-more-shocking.html.

2) Judson Phillips, "The State of the Union: Liberals Are the New Nazis," *Tea Party Nation*, posted February 12, 2013, accessed March 28, 2016, http://www.teapartynation.com/forum/topics/the-state-of-the-union-liberals-are-the-new-nazis.

3) Oliver Willis, "ADL Criticizes "Inappropriate" Holocaust References from Conservative Media During Gun Debate," *Media Matters for America*, posted January 24, 2013, accessed March 28, 2016, http://mediamatters.org/blog/2013/01/24/adl-criticizes-inappropriate-holocaust-referenc/192383.

4) R. J. Johnson, "Barack O'Hitler—The Right Wing's Favorite Past Time Debunked," *The Political Garbage Chute*, posted January 28, 2013, accessed March 28, 2016, http://www.politicalgarbagechute.com/barack-ohitler-the-right-wings-favorite-past-time-debunked/.

5) Ibid.

6) "ADL Urges Dems to Stop Making Nazi and Holocaust Comparisons," *Newsmax*, posted September 6, 2012, accessed March 28, 2016, http://www.newsmax.com/Newsfront/adl-democrats-nazi-comparisons/2012/09/06/id/450928#ixzz2L6LfH9qN.

7) In conversation with Jewish psychologists Dawn Menken, Ph.D., author of *Raising Parents, Raising Kids: Hands-on Wisdom for the Next Generation*, and Gary Reiss, Ph.D., author of *Beyond War and Peace in the Arab Israeli Conflict*.

8) Ibid.

9) Ibid.

10) Ibid.

8. I'm Not a Hypochondriac — I'm Just a Jew

1) Woody Allen, "Hypochondria: An Inside Look," *NYTimes.com*, posted January 12, 2013, accessed March 17, 2015, http://www.nytimes.com/2013/01/13/opinion/sunday/hypochondria-an-inside-look.html?_r=2.

10. Paging Dr. Ben Carson: Homophobia Calling

1) Carl Jung, "The Philosophical Tree," *Collected Works 13: Alchemical Studies* (1945), 335.

2) Tessa Berenson, "Ben Carson Apologizes for Saying Prison Makes People Gay," *Time.com*, posted March 5, 2015, accessed September 25, 2015 http://time.com/3733184/ben-carson-gay-prison/.

3) Fanny Moser, *Spuk: Irrglaube oder Wahrglaube?* Foreword by C. G Jung (Zurich: Gyr-Verlag, 1950), 10.

4) Timothy J. Dailey, "Homosexuality and Child Sexual Abuse," *OrthodoxyToday.org*, accessed March 28, 2016, http://www.orthodoxytoday.org/articles/DaileyHomosexualAbuse.php?/articles/DaileyHomosexualAbuse.htm.

5) Judith M. Glassgold, Lee Beckstead, Jack Drescher, Beverly Greene, Robin Lin Miller, and Roger L. Worthington, "Report of the American Psychological Association Task Force on Appropriate Therapeutic Response to Sexual Orientation," *American Psychological Association*, posted August 2009, accessed March 28, 2016, http://www.apa.org/pi/lgbt/resources/therapeutic-response.pdf, 11.

6) Jerome Hunt and Aisha C. Moodie-Mills, "The Unfair Criminalization of Gay and Transgender Youth," *Center for American Progress*, posted June 29, 2012, accessed March 28, 2016, https://www.americanprogress.org/issues/lgbt/report/2012/06/29/11730/the-unfair-criminalization-of-gay-and-transgender-youth/.

7) Katy, "The Problem with the Belief that Child Sexual Abuse *Causes* Homosexuality / Bisexuality," *Pandora's Project*, posted 2009, accessed March 28, 2016, http://www.pandys.org/articles/abuseandhomosexuality.html.

8) Jerome Hunt and Aisha C. Moodie-Mills, "The Unfair Criminalization of Gay and Transgender Youth," *Center for American Progress*, posted June 29, 2012, accessed March 28, 2016, https://www.americanprogress.org/issues/lgbt/report/2012/06/29/11730/the-unfair-criminalization-of-gay-and-transgender-youth/.

9) Ibid.

10) David Gibson, "Five Myths About the Catholic Sexual Abuse Scandal," *WashingtonPost.com*, posted April 18, 2010, accessed March 28, 2016, http://www.washingtonpost.com/wp-dyn/content/article/2010/04/16/AR2010041602026.html.

11) Gregory Herek, "Facts About Homosexuality and Child Molestation," *Sexual Orientation: Science, Education, and Policy,* accessed March 28,

2016, http://psc.dss.ucdavis.edu/rainbow/HTML/facts_molestation. html.

12) Nanette K. Gartrell, Henny M. W. Bos, and Naomi G. Goldberg, "Adolescents of the U.S. National Longitudinal Lesbian Family Study: Sexual Orientation, Sexual Behavior, and Sexual Risk Exposure," *National Longitudinal Lesbian Family Study*, posted June 4, 2010, accessed March 28, 2016, https://www.nllfs.org/images/uploads/ pdf/NLLFS-adolescents-sexuality-2010.pdf.

13) "Brené Brown on Shame: 'It Cannot Survive Empathy'" *The Huffington Post*, posted August 26, 2013, accessed March 28, 2016, http://www. huffingtonpost.com/2013/08/26/brene-brown-shame_n_3807115. html.

14) Laura Kann, Emily O'Malley Olsen, Tim McManus, Steve Kinchen, David Chyen, William A. Harris, and Howell Wechsler, "Sexual Identity, Sex of Sexual Contacts, and Health-Risk Behaviors Among Students in Grades 9-12: Youth Risk Behavior Surveillance, Selected Sites, United States, 2001-2009," *Division of Adolescent and School Health, National Center for Chronic Disease Prevention and Health Promotion, CDC*, posted June 10, 2011, accessed March 28, 2016, http://www.cdc.gov/mmwr/preview/mmwrhtml/ss6007a1.htm.

Section II
Hunger, Self-Hatred, Failure and Sexism:
The Real Weight-Loss Story

1. Does America Really Need to Go on a Diet?

1) Liz Neporent, "Childhood Obesity: Is 7 Too Young to Diet?" *ABCNews.com*, posted March 12, 2013, accessed February 15, 2016, http://abcnews.go.com/Health/childhood-obesity-young-diet/ story?id=18704647&page=2.

2) "Childhood Obesity Facts," *Centers for Disease Control and Prevention*, posted August 27, 2015, accessed February 15, 2016, http://www.cdc. gov/healthyyouth/obesity/facts.htm.

3) "Overweight and Obesity Statistics," *National Institute of Diabetes and Digestive and Kidney Diseases,* posted October 2012, accessed February 15, 2016, http://win.niddk.nih.gov/statistics/index.htm.

4) Cheryl D. Fryar, Margaret D. Carroll, and Cynthia L. Ogden, "Prevalence of Obesity Among Children and Adolescents: United States, Trends 1963-1965 Through 2009-2010," *Centers for Disease Control and Prevention*, posted November 6, 2015, accessed March 21, 2016, http://www.cdc.gov/nchs/data/hestat/obesity_child_09_10/obesity_child_09_10.htm.

5) S. W. McNutt, Y. Hu, G. B. Schreiber, P. B. Crawford, E. Obarzanek, and L. Mellin, "A Longitudinal Study of the Dietary Practices of Black and White Girls 9 and 10 Years Old at Enrollment: The NHLBI Growth and Health Study," *Journal of Adolescent Health*, 20, no. 1 (1997): 27-37.

6) Katherine M. Flegal, Brian K. Kit, Heather Orpana, and Barry I. Graubard, "Association of All-Cause Mortality with Overweight and Obesity Using Standard Body Mass Index Categories: A Systemic Review and Meta-analysis," *The Journal of the American Medical Association*, 309, no. 1 (2013): 71-82.

7) Glenn A. Gaesser, *Big Fat Lies: The Truth About Your Weight and Your Health* (Carlsbad, CA: Gürze Books, 2002 [1996]), 77.

8) Shaun Dreisbach, "Shocking Body-Image News: 97% of Women Will Be Cruel to Their Bodies Today," *Glamour.com*, posted February 3, 2011, accessed January 16, 2013, http://www.glamour.com/health-fitness/2011/02/shocking-body-image-news-97-percent-of-women-will-be-cruel-to-their-bodies-today?currentPage=2 - The Real (Really Harsh) Things Women Think About Their Bodies.

9) Lisa Berzins, "Dying to Be Thin: The Prevention of Eating Disorders and The Role of Federal Policy. APA Co-Sponsored Congressional Briefing," USA, November 1997.

10) "Eating Disorder Statistics," *South Carolina Department of Mental Health*, accessed March 28, 2016, http://www.state.sc.us/dmh/anorexia/statistics.htm.

11) "Obesity and Mortality," *Obesity: Facts, Figures, Guidelines*, accessed March 28, 2016, http://www.wvdhhr.org/bph/oehp/obesity/mortality.htm.

12) Ibid.

13) "Consequences of Eating Disorders," *Eating Disorder Foundation of Orange County*, accessed March 28, 2016, http://www.edfoc.org/consequences-eating-disorders/.

14) Brooke Axtell, "How to Be a Shameless Woman: Making Peace with Our Bodies, Ourselves," *Forbes.com*, posted September 26, 2012, accessed March 23, 2016, http://www.forbes.com/sites/shenegotiates/2012/09/26/how-to-be-a-shameless-woman-making-peace-with-our-bodies-ourselves/.

15) Shari Roan, "Keeping It Off," *LATimes.com*, posted June 2, 2008, accessed March 21, 2016, http://articles.latimes.com/2008/jun/02/health/ he-regain2.

3. Why Diets Fail: Seven Things You Should Know

1) Amanda Spake, "Stop Dieting! Forget the Scale, the Calorie Counting, and Forbidden Foods. They May Be Doing More Harm Than Good," *USNews.com*, posted January 8, 2006, accessed October 31, 2011, http://health.usnews.com/usnews/health/articles/060116/ 16diet. htm (page since deleted).

2) Glenn A. Gaesser, *Big Fat Lies: The Truth About Your Weight and Your Health* (Carlsbad, CA: Gürze Books, 2002 [1996]), 77.

3) Traci Mann, A. Janet Tomiyama, Erika Westling, Ann-Marie Lew, Barbra Samuels, and Jason Chatman, "Medicare's Search for Effective Obesity Treatments: Diets Are Not the Answer," *American Psychologist*, 62, no. 3 (2007): 220–233.

5. Shame, Body Image, and Weight Loss

1) University of Nebraska-Lincoln, "How Our Brains See Men as People and Women as Body Parts: Both Genders Process Images of Men, Women Differently," *Science Daily*, posted July 25, 2012, accessed March 23, 2016, www.sciencedaily.com/releases/2012/07/120725150215.htm.

2) Shaun Dreisbach, "Shocking Body-Image News: 97% of Women Will Be Cruel to Their Bodies Today," *Glamour.com*, posted February 3, 2011,

accessed January 16, 2013, http://www.glamour.com/health-fitness/ 2011/02/shocking-body-image-news-97-percent-of-women-will-be-cruel-to-their-bodies-today?currentPage=2 - The Real (Really Harsh) Things Women Think About Their Bodies.

3) Carolyn Coker Ross, "Why Do Women Hate Their Bodies?" *PsychCentral. com*, posted June 1, 2012, accessed January 16, 2013, http://psychcentral. com/ blog/archives/2012/06/02/why-do-women-hate-their-bodies/.

4) "Overweight Brides," *Dr. Phil*, CBS, January 12, 2005.

5) Ross, "Why Do Women Hate Their Bodies?"

6) Katherine M. Flegal, Brian K. Kit, Heather Orpana, and Barry I. Graubard, "Association of All-Cause Mortality With Overweight and Obesity Using Standard Body Mass Index Categories: A Systematic Review and Meta-analysis." *The Journal of the American Medical Association,* 309, no. 1 (2013): 71-82.

7) Glenn A. Gaesser, *Big Fat Lies: The Truth About Your Weight and Your Health* (Carlsbad, CA: Gürze Books, 2002 [1996]), 77.

6. Resolving to Lose Weight? Consider This First

1) Brooke Axtell, "How to Be a Shameless Woman: Making Peace with Our Bodies, Ourselves," *Forbes.com*, posted September 26, 2012, accessed March 23, 2016, http://www.forbes.com/sites/shenegotiates/2012/ 09/26/how-to-be-a-shameless-woman-making-peace-with-our-bodies-ourselves/.

Section III

What's Going On? Reflections on Current Events

2. Diagnosing Depression in the Wake of Robin Williams's Suicide

1) Richard Bentall and Nick Craddock, "Do We Need a Diagnostic Manual for Mental Illness?" *The Guardian*, posted February 10, 2012, accessed March 28, 2016, http://www.theguardian.com/commentisfree/2012/ feb/10/diagnostic-manual-mental-illness.

2) Erving Goffman, *Stigma: Notes on the Management of Spoiled Identity* (Englewood Cliffs, NJ: Prentice Hall, 1963): 3.

3) Bruce G. Link and Jo C. Phelan, "Conceptualizing Stigma," *Annual Review of Sociology*, 27 (2001): 363–385.

4) Linda Garand, Jennifer H. Lingler, Kyaien O. Conner, and Mary Amanda Dew, "Diagnostic Labels, Stigma, and Participation in Research Related to Dementia and Mild Cognitive Impairment," *Research in Gerontological Nursing*, 2, no. 2 (2009): 112-121.

5) Jerry Kennard, "The Pros and Cons of a Psychiatric Diagnosis," *Health Central*, posted October 13, 2013, accessed March 28, 2016, http://www.healthcentral.com/depression/c/4182/163428/cons-psychiatric-diagnosis/.

6) Salvador Minuchin, *Families and Family Therapy* (Cambridge, MA: Harvard University Press, 1974).

7) James Weeks, "Crazy or Not Crazy?" *Across the King's River*, posted June 17, 2014, accessed March 28, 2016, http://www.acrossthekingsriver.com/crazy-or-not-crazy/.

8) Ibid.

9) Bernard Lo and Marilyn J. Field, eds., *Conflict of Interest in Medical Research, Education, and Practice* (Washington, DC: Institute of Medicine of the National Academies Press, 2009), accessed March 28, 2016, http://www.ncbi.nlm.nih.gov/books/NBK22942/pdf/Bookshelf_NBK22942.pdf.

10) Craig J. Whittington, Tim Kendall, Peter Fonagy, David Cottrell, Andrew Cotgrove, and Ellen Boddington, "Selective Serotonin Reuptake Inhibitors in Childhood Depression: Systematic Review of Published Versus Unpublished Data," *The Lancet*, 363, no. 9418 (2004): 1341–1345, accessed March 28, 2016, http://www.thelancet.com/pdfs/journals/lancet/PIIS0140673604160431.pdf.

11) Erick H. Turner, Annette M. Matthews, Eftihia Linardatos, Robert A. Tell, and Robert Rosenthal, "Selective Publication of Antidepressant Trials and Its Influence on Apparent Efficacy," *The New England Journal of Medicine*, 358, no. 3 (2008), accessed March 28, 2016, http://www.nejm.org/doi/full/10.1056/NEJMsa065779.

3. The Lie of Brian (Williams)

1) Julie Diamond, "Scary. Scarier. Scariest," *Julie Diamond* (blog), posted January 23, 2013, accessed March 28, 2016, http://juliediamond.net/home-page-blog/scary-scarier-scariest/.

2) "Eating Disorders Statistics," *Anorexia Nervosa and Associated Disorders*, accessed March 28, 2016, http://www.anad.org/get-information/about-eating-disorders/eating-disorders-statistics/.

3) D. Hagar, "People Pleaser," *Urban Dictionary*, posted May 22, 2013, accessed March 28, 2016, http://www.urbandictionary.com/define.php?term=people+pleaser.

4) "Cheating Is a Personal Foul," *The Educational Testing Service / Ad Council Campaign to Discourage Academic Cheating*, 1999, accessed March 15, 2015, http://www.glass-castle.com/clients/www-nocheating-org/adcouncil/research/cheatingfactsheet.html.

5) Susan Donaldson James, "Honeymoon with Viagra Could Be over, Say Doctors," *ABCNews.com*, posted June 9, 2011, accessed March 28, 2016, http://abcnews.go.com/Health/viagra-prescription-sales-sexual-expectations/story?id=13794726.

6) Benedict Carey, "Denial Makes the World Go Round," *NYTimes.com*, posted November 20, 2007, accessed March 28, 2016, http://www.nytimes.com/2007/11/20/health/research/20deni.html?pagewanted=all&_r=0.

7) Jamelle Bouie, "The New Racism: First You Deny Racism Exists," *ChicagoTribune.com*, posted September 8, 2014, accessed March 28, 2016, http://www.chicagotribune.com/news/opinion/commentary/chi-racism-america-michael-brown-trayvon-martin-20140908-story.html#page=1.

4. Who Cheats? Who Lies? Moving Beyond Lance Armstrong

1) Josh Ritchie, "20 Tax Facts that Will Astonish You," *TurboTax Blog*, posted July 13, 2011, accessed March 28, 2016, http://blog.turbotax.intuit.com/tax-news/20-tax-facts-that-will-astonish-you-6665/.

2) "Facts and Statistics About Infidelity," *Truth About Deception*, accessed March 28, 2016, http://www.truthaboutdeception.com/cheating-and-infidelity/stats-about-infidelity.html.

3) "Cheating Is a Personal Foul," *The Educational Testing Service / Ad Council Campaign to Discourage Academic Cheating*, 1999, accessed March 15, 2015, http://www.glass-castle.com/clients/www-nocheating-org/adcouncil/research/cheatingfactsheet.html.

4) Julie Diamond, "Scary. Scarier. Scariest," *Julie Diamond* (blog), posted January 23, 2013, accessed March 28, 2016, http://juliediamond.net/home-page-blog/scary-scarier-scariest/.

5) Lisa King, "The Doping of America, Part 2: The Ritalin Generation," *Appalachian Chronicles*, posted June 24, 2012, accessed March 28, 2016, http://www.childrensbehaviorproblems.com/doping-american-kid-medicated-world/.

6) "Cheating Is a Personal Foul."

7) Ibid.

8) Rome Neal, "Caffeine Nation," *CBSNews.com*, posted November 14, 2002, accessed March 15, 2015, http://www.cbsnews.com/news/caffeine-nation/.

9) Ibid.

10) "1-In-5 Young Women Using Diet Pills," *Aphrodite Women's Health*, posted November 1, 2006, accessed March 28, 2016, http://www.aphroditewomenshealth.com/news/20061001001445_health_news.shtml.

11) Susan Donaldson James, "Honeymoon with Viagra Could Be Over, Say Doctors," *ABCNews.com*, posted June 9, 2011, accessed March 15, 2015, http://abcnews.go.com/Health/viagra-prescription-sales-sexual-expectations/story?id=13794726.

5. Upon the Murder of 20 Children and 6 Adults in Connecticut

1) James Baldwin, *The Fire Next Time* (New York: Vintage, 1991 [1962]), 5–6.

2) Cornel West, *Hope on a Tightrope: Words & Wisdom* (Carlsbad, CA: Hay House, 2008), 29.

10. In Honor of Maya Angelou: This Caged Bird Sang and Sang

1) Mary Jane Lupton, *Maya Angelou: A Critical Companion* (Westport, CT: Greenwood: 1998), 5.

2) "Maya Angelou Biography," *Academy of Achievement*, posted May 28, 2014, accessed March 28, 2016, http://www.achievement.org/autodoc/page/angobio-1.

3) Maya Angelou, *I Know Why the Caged Bird Sings* (New York: Bantam Books, 1969).

4) "Dr. Maya Angelou—I Am Human," *YouTube*, posted March 4, 2013, accessed March 28, 2016, https://www.youtube.com/watch?v=ePodNjrVSsk.

5) Cornel West, *Restoring Hope: Conversations on the Future of Black America* (Boston: Beacon Press, 1997), 199.

S e c t i o n   I V
Beyond a Popular Psychology: Remembering the Shadow

1. Into the Dark: A Psychology of Soul, Shadow, and Diversity

1) Mandy Silver, "Cornel West Delivers 'Inspiring' Lecture," *Student Life*, posted February 3, 2006, accessed March 8, 2016, http://www.studlife.com/archives/News/2006/02/03/CornelWestdeliversinspiringlecture/.

3. Six Reasons Not to Forgive — Not Yet

1) Laura B. Luchies, Eli J. Finkel, James K. McNulty, Madoka Kumashiro, "The Doormat Effect: When Forgiving Erodes Self-Respect and Self-Concept Clarity," *Journal of Personality and Social Psychology*, 98 (2010): 734–749.

2) James K. McNulty, "The Dark Side of Forgiveness: The Tendency to Forgive Predicts Continued Psychological and Physical Aggression in Marriage," *Personality and Social Psychology Bulletin*, 37 (June 2011): 770-783.

3) William H. Grier and Price M. Cobbs, *Black Rage* (Eugene, OR: Wipf & Stock Publishers, 2000).

4. Understanding Stress: Beyond Reduction, Management, and Coping

1) "Stress Symptoms: Effects on Your Body and Behavior," *Mayo Clinic*, posted July 19, 2013, accessed May 15, 2015, http://www.mayoclinic.org/healthy-living/stress-management/in-depth/stress-symptoms/art-20050987. See also: Brian Krans, "8 Ways Stress Is More Dangerous Than You Think," *Healthline News*, posted August 27, 2013, accessed March 15, 2015, http://www.healthline.com/health-news/mental-eight-ways-stress-harms-your-health-082713.

2) Hans Selye, "Stress, in Addition to Being Itself, Was Also the Cause of Itself, and the Result of Itself," *The American Institute of Stress*, accessed March 15, 2015, http://www.stress.org/management-tips/#sthash.i9jqbZUu.dpuf. See also: "Stress Management Health Center: Reducing Stress, Stress Symptoms, Causes, Treatments, and Relief," *WebMD*, posted March 15, 2015, http://www.webmd.com/balance/stress-management/.

3) See for example, one of the best-studied stress-relievers, the relaxation response, first described by Harvard's Herbert Benson, M.D. from The American Institute of Stress. Herbert Benson, "Steps to Elicit the Relaxation Response," *Relaxation Response*, accessed March 15, 2015, http://www.relaxationresponse.org/steps/.

4) Lisa Belkin, "HuffPost Survey Reveals Lack of Sleep As A Major Cause of Stress Among Americans," *The Huffington Post*, posted May 24, 2013, accessed March 15, 2015, http://www.huffingtonpost.com/2013/04/29/stress-survey-sleep_n_3156991.html.

5) "Brain Basics: Understanding Sleep," *National Institute of Neurological Disorders and Stroke,* updated July 25, 2014, accessed March 15, 2015, http://www.ninds.nih.gov/disorders/brain_basics/understanding_sleep.htm.

6) Ibid.

7) Ibid.

8) "Sleep Tips: 7 Steps to Better Sleep," *Mayo Clinic*, posted June 9, 2014, accessed March 15, 2015, http://www.mayoclinic.org/healthy-living/adult-health/in-depth/sleep/art-20048379?pg=1.

9) Shari Roan, "Keeping It Off," *LATimes.com*, posted June 2, 2008, accessed March 15, 2015, http://articles.latimes.com/2008/jun/02/health/he-regain2.

10) Shaun Dreisbach, "Shocking Body-Image News: 97% of Women Will Be Cruel to Their Bodies Today," *Glamour.com*, posted February 3, 2011, accessed March 15, 2015, http://www.glamour.com/health-fitness/2011/02/shocking-body-image-news-97-percent-of-women-will-be-cruel-to-their-bodies-today/2#The%20Real%20%28Really%20Harsh%29%20Things%20Women%20Think%20About%20Their%20Bodies.

11) Lottie L. Joiner, "Black May Not Crack, but We're Aging Faster Inside," *The Root*, posted November 30, 2013, accessed October 1, 2015, http://www.theroot.com/articles/uncategorized/2013/11/black_women_and_health_extreme_stress_causes_accelerated_biological_aging/.

12) Ibid.

13) Karina L. Walters and Jane M. Simoni, "Reconceptualizing Native Women's Health: An "Indigenist" Stress-Coping Model," *American Journal of Public Health*, 92, no. 4 (2002): 520-524.

6. Resolutions, Commitments, and All That Jazz: Five Reasons Why Resolutions Fail

1) "Mindfulness: Present Moment Awareness," *PsychologyToday.com*, accessed March 21, 2016, http://www.psychologytoday.com/basics/mindfulness.

9. What Is Shame? How Does It Color Our World?

1) While the abuse of a child is only one of many situations where insufficient witnessing leads to shame, I use this example because it is familiar and easily understood.

10. When "Questions" Shame: Learning to Be More Direct

1) Amy Mindell, "Amy on the Evolution of Process Theory," *Amy and Arnold Mindell* (website), posted Fall 2002, accessed March 21, 2016, http://www.aamindell.net/1710/worldwork-terms/double-signals/.

11. Beyond Individual Psychology: How Psychology Shames

1)   Arnold Mindell, *City Shadows: Psychological Interventions in Psychiatry* (Portland, OR: Lao Tse Press, 2009).

12. Winning the Battle with Inner Criticism

1)   Weekend Edition Sunday, "At 80, Maya Angelou Reflects on a 'Glorious' Life," *NPR.org*, posted April 6, 2008, accessed April 5, 2016, http://www.npr.org/2008/04/06/89355359/at-80-maya-angelou-reflects-on-a-glorious-life.

13. Understanding Dreams About Inner and Outer Criticism

1)   "Facts About Suicide," *The Trevor Project* (website), accessed April 5, 2016, http://www.thetrevorproject.org/pages/facts-about-suicide.

2)   "Idiom: Death of a Thousand Cuts," *UsingEnglish.com*, accessed April 5, 2016, http://www.usingenglish.com/reference/idioms/death+of+a+thousand+cuts.html.

14. Getting Real: Seven Roadblocks to Becoming Our Authentic Selves

1)   D. W. Winnicott, "Ego Distortion in Terms of True and False Self," *The Maturational Process and the Facilitating Environment: Studies in the Theory of Emotional Development* (New York: International UP Inc., 1965): 140–152.

2)   Tian Dayton, "Creating A False Self: Learning To Live A Lie," *The Huffington Post*, posted November 17, 2011, accessed March 8, 2016, http://www.huffingtonpost.com/dr-tian-dayton/creating-a-false-self-lea_b_269096.html.

3)   Noel L. Griese, "The Bible vs. Mao: A "Best Guess" of the Top 25 Best-selling Books of All Time," *Publishing Perspectives*, posted September 7, 2010, accessed March 8, 2016, http://publishingperspectives.com/2010/09/top-25-bestselling-books-of-all-time/.

4)   John Gray, *Men Are from Mars, Women Are from Venus: A Practical Guide for Improving Communication and Getting What You Want in Your Relationships* (New York: HarperCollins, 1992).

5) Arlene Skolnick, *The Intimate Environment: Exploring Marriage and the Family*, 5th ed. (New York: HarperCollins, 1992), 190.

6) J. Kenneth Davidson and Nelwyn B. Moore, *Marriage and Family: Change and Community* (Boston: Allyn & Bacon, 1996), 86.

7) Warren Throckmorton, "Mark Driscoll's Real Marriage and Robert Brannon's Male Sex Roles: Coincidence or Something More?" *Patheos*, posted January 23, 2014, accessed March 21, 2016, http://www.patheos. com/blogs/warrenthrockmorton/2014/01/23/mark-driscolls-real-marriage-and-robert-brannons-male-sex-roles-coincidence-or-something-more/.

8) John Thomas Didymus, "Growing Number of Young Men Are Getting Addicted to Viagra," *Digital Journal,* posted October 4, 2012, accessed March 22, 2016, http://www.digitaljournal.com/article/ 334150.

9) Lea Winerman, "Helping Men to Help Themselves," *American Psychological Association*, posted June 2005, accessed March 22, 2016, http://www.apa.org/monitor/jun05/helping.aspx.

10) Suzanne Goldenberg, "Why Women Are Poor at Science, by Harvard President," *The Guardian*, posted January 18, 2005, accessed March 22, 2016, http://www.theguardian.com/science/2005/jan/18/educationsgendergap.genderissues.

11) Thomas A. Kochan, "Microsoft CEO's Advice On Pay Raises Is Wrong For All (Not Just Women)," *Fortune.com*, posted October 27, 2014, accessed March 23, 2016, http://fortune.com/2014/10/27/microsoft-ceos-advice-on-pay-raises-is-wrong-for-all-not-just-women/.

12) Maya Angelou, "On the Pulse of Morning," *Poem Hunter*, accessed March 23, 2016, http://www.poemhunter.com/poem/on-the-pulse-of-morning/.

13) Joshua Garriga, "Cornel West, Harvard, and the Pursuit of Greatness," *The Daily Garriga* (blog), posted November 12, 2011, accessed March 23, 2016, http://thedailygarriga.com/2011/11/12/cornel-west-harvard-and-the-pursuit-of-greatness/.

14) Zhong, Chen-Bo, "The Ethical Dangers of Rational Decision Making,"

Academy of Management Proceedings, posted August 1, 2008, accessed March 23, 2016, http://proceedings.aom.org/content/2008/1/1.270.full.pdf+html.

15) Melissa Dahl, "The Alarming New Research on Perfectionism," *NYMag.com*, posted September 30, 2014, accessed March 23, 2016, http://nymag.com/scienceofus/2014/09/alarming-new-research-on-perfectionism.html.

16) Gerald Wiviott, "The Psychology of Fundamentalism," accessed March 23, 2016, http://infosect.freeshell.org/infocult/The_Psychology_of_Fundamentalism-Gerald_Wiviott.pdf.

17) Ibid.

15. The Courage to Find Soul: A Call for More "Psyche" in Psychology

1) John Larosa, "U.S. Weight Loss Market Worth $60.9 Billion," *PRWeb*, posted May 9, 2011, accessed March 8, 2016, http://www.prweb.com/releases/2011/5/prweb8393658.htm.

Bibliography

"1-In-5 Young Women Using Diet Pills." *Aphrodite Women's Health.* Posted November 1, 2006. Accessed March 28, 2016. http://www. aphroditewomenshealth.com /news/20061001001445_health_news. shtml.

"ADL Urges Dems to Stop Making Nazi and Holocaust Comparisons." *Newsmax.* Posted September 6, 2012. Accessed March 28, 2016. http:// www.newsmax.com/Newsfront/adl-democrats-nazi-comparisons/ 2012/09/06/id/450928#ixzz2L6LfH9qN.

Allen, Woody. "Hypochondria: An Inside Look." *NYTimes.com.* Posted January 12, 2013. Accessed March 17, 2015. http://www.nytimes.com/ 2013/01/13/opinion/sunday/hypochondria-an-inside-look.html?_r=2.

Angelou, Maya. *I Know Why the Caged Bird Sings.* New York: Bantam Books, 1969.

———. "On the Pulse of Morning." *Poem Hunter.* Accessed March 23, 2016. http://www.poemhunter.com/poem/on-the-pulse-of-morning/.

Axtell, Brooke. "How to Be a Shameless Woman: Making Peace with Our Bodies, Ourselves." *Forbes.com.* Posted September 26, 2012. Accessed March 23, 2016. http://www.forbes.com/sites/shenegotiates/2012/09/ 26/how-to-be-a-shameless-woman-making-peace-with-our-bodies-ourselves/.

Baldwin, James. *The Fire Next Time.* New York: The Dial Press, 1963.

Beckett, Katherine and Heather Evans. "The Role of Race in Washington State Capital Sentencing 1981-2012." *Death Penalty Information Center.* Posted January 27, 2014. Accessed March 28, 2016. http://www.deathpenaltyinfo.org/documents/WashRaceStudy2014.pdf.

Bedrick, David. *Talking Back to Dr. Phil: Alternatives to Mainstream Psychology.* Santa Fe, NM: Belly Song Press, 2013.

Belkin, Lisa. "HuffPost Survey Reveals Lack of Sleep As A Major Cause of Stress Among Americans." *The Huffington Post.* Posted May 24, 2013. Accessed March 15, 2015. http://www.huffingtonpost.com/2013/04/29/stress-survey-sleep_n_3156991.html.

Benson, Herbert. "Steps to Elicit the Relaxation Response." *Relaxation Response.* Accessed March 15, 2015. http://www.relaxationresponse.org/steps/.

Bentall, Richard and Nick Craddock. "Do We Need a Diagnostic Manual for Mental Illness?" *The Guardian.* Posted February 10, 2012. Accessed March 28, 2016. http://www.theguardian.com/commentisfree/2012/feb/10/diagnostic-manual-mental-illness.

Berenson, Tessa. "Ben Carson Apologizes for Saying Prison Makes People Gay." *Time.com.* Posted March 5, 2015. Accessed September 25, 2015. http://time.com/3733184/ben-carson-gay-prison/.

Bertrand, Marianne. "Racial Bias in Hiring: Are Emily and Brendan More Employable than Lakisha and Jamal." *The University of Chicago Graduate School of Business,* 4, no. 4 (2003). Accessed March 28, 2016. http://www.chicagobooth.edu/capideas/spring03/racialbias.html.

Berzins, Lisa. "Dying to Be Thin: The Prevention of Eating Disorders and The Role of Federal Policy. APA Co-Sponsored Congressional Briefing." USA. November 1997.

Biema, David Van. "Mother Teresa's Crisis of Faith." *Time.com.* Posted August 23, 2007. Accessed March 17, 2015. http://content.time.com/time/magazine/article/0,9171,1655720,00.html.

Black Lives Matter. Accessed August 15, 2015. http://blacklivesmatter.com.

Blake, Heidi. "Why Women Think They Are Fat: Brain 'Thinks Body Is Two Thirds Bigger Than It Is.'" *The Telegraph.* Posted June 15, 2010.

Accessed on March 21, 2016. http://www.telegraph.co.uk/news/health/ news/7826822/Why-women-think-they-are-fat-brain-thinks-body-is-two-thirds-bigger-than-it-is.html.

Bouie, Jamelle. "The Gulf that Divides Us." *Slate*. Posted October 17, 2014. Accessed February 2, 2016. http://www.slate.com/articles/news_ and_politics/politics/2014/10/the_whiteness_project_whites_and_ blacks_are_still_living_in_separate_worlds.html.

———. "The New Racism: First You Deny Racism Exists." *ChicagoTribune. com*. Posted September 8, 2014. Accessed March 28, 2016. http:// www.chicagotribune.com/news/opinion/commentary/chi-racism-america-michael-brown-trayvon-martin-20140908-story.html #page=1.

Boynton, Robert S. "Detour to the Promised Land." *NYTimes.com*. Posted January 23, 2000. Accessed March 17, 2015. http://www.nytimes.com/ books/00/01/23/reviews/000123.23boynt.html.

"Brain Basics: Understanding Sleep." *National Institute of Neurological Disorders and Stroke*. Updated July 25, 2014. Accessed March 15, 2015. http://www.ninds.nih.gov/disorders/brain_basics/understanding_ sleep.htm.

"Brené Brown on Shame: 'It Cannot Survive Empathy.'" *The Huffington Post*. Posted August 26, 2013. Accessed March 28, 2016. http://www. huffingtonpost.com/2013/08/26/brene-brown-shame_n_3807115. html.

Brown, Gita. "Segregation Is Back in America's Public School." *Rhode Island College*. Posted November 2, 2009. Accessed March 17, 2015. http://www.ric.edu/news/details.php?News_ID=652.

Campbell, Andy. "Florida Cops Fired over Racist Texts, KKK Video." *The Huffington Post*. Posted March 22, 2015. Accessed February 2, 2016. http://www.huffingtonpost.com/2015/03/22/cops-fired-racist-video_n_6918652.html?fb_action_ids=824529154261943&fb_ action_types=og.comments.

Carey, Benedict. "Denial Makes the World Go Round." *NYTimes.com*. Posted November 20, 2007. Accessed March 28, 2016. http://www.

nytimes.com/2007/11/20/health/research/20deni.html?pagewanted
=all&_r=0.

"Cheating Is a Personal Foul." *The Educational Testing Service / Ad Council
Campaign to Discourage Academic Cheating.* 1999. Accessed March 15,
2015. http://www.glass-castle.com/clients/www-nocheating-org/
adcouncil/research/cheatingfactsheet.html.

"Childhood Obesity Facts." *Centers for Disease Control and Prevention.*
Posted August 27, 2015. Accessed February 15, 2016. http://www.cdc.
gov/healthyyouth/obesity/facts.htm.

"Consequences of Eating Disorders." *Eating Disorder Foundation of
Orange County.* Accessed March 28, 2016. http://www.edfoc.org/
consequences-eating-disorders/.

Craig, W. J., ed. "Sonnet 29." *The Complete Works of William Shakespeare.*
London: Oxford University Press, 1914. Accessed May 10, 2016.
http://www.bartleby.com/70/50029.html.

Dahl, Melissa. "The Alarming New Research on Perfectionism." *NYMag.
com.* Posted September 30, 2014. Accessed March 23, 2016. http://
nymag.com/scienceofus/2014/09/alarming-new-research-on-
perfectionism.html.

Dailey, Timothy J. "Homosexuality and Child Sexual Abuse."
OrthodoxyToday.org. Accessed March 28, 2016. http://www.
orthodoxytoday.org/articles/DaileyHomosexualAbuse.php?/
articles/DaileyHomosexualAbuse.htm.

Davidson, J. Kenneth and Nelwyn B. Moore. *Marriage and Family: Change
and Community.* Boston: Allyn & Bacon, 1996.

Dayton, Tian. "Creating A False Self: Learning To Live A Lie." *The
Huffington Post.* Posted November 17, 2011. Accessed March 8, 2016.
http://www.huffingtonpost.com/dr-tian-dayton/creating-a-false-
self-lea_b_269096.html.

Death Penalty Information Center. Accessed August 15, 2015. http://www.
deathpenaltyinfo.org/race-and-death-penalty.

Denvir, Daniel. "Meet MLK's Glenn Beck-Loving Niece." *Salon.* Posted
August 27, 2010. Accessed January 13, 2013. http://www.salon.com/
2010/08/27/alveda_king_glenn_beck/.

Diamond, Julie. "Scary. Scarier. Scariest." *Julie Diamond* (blog). Posted January 23, 2013. Accessed March 28, 2016. http://juliediamond.net/home-page-blog/scary-scarier-scariest/.

Didymus, John Thomas. "Growing Number of Young Men Are Getting Addicted to Viagra." *Digital Journal.* Posted October 4, 2012. Accessed March 22, 2016. http://www.digitaljournal.com/article/334150.

"Discount Babies." *Economist.com.* Posted May 14, 2010. Accessed August 15, 2015. http://www.economist.com/blogs/freeexchange/2010/05/markets_everything.

Dreisbach, Shaun. "Shocking Body-Image News: 97% of Women Will Be Cruel to Their Bodies Today." *Glamour.com.* Posted February 3, 2011. Accessed January 16, 2013. http://www.glamour.com/health-fitness/2011/02/shocking-body-image-news-97-percent-of-women-will-be-cruel-to-their-bodies-today?currentPage=2 - The Real (Really Harsh) Things Women Think About Their Bodies.

"Dr. Maya Angelou—I Am Human." *YouTube.* Posted March 4, 2013. Accessed March 28, 2016. https://www.youtube.com/watch?v=ePodNjrVSsk.

"Du Bois and the Question of the Color Line: Race and Class in the Age of Globalization." *Journal of the Research Group on Socialism and Democracy Online.* Posted April 19, 2011. Accessed March 28, 2016. http://sdonline.org/33/du-bois-and-the-question-of-the-color-line-race-and-class-in-the-age-of-globalization/.

"Eating Disorders Statistics." *Anorexia Nervosa and Associated Disorders.* Accessed March 28, 2016. http://www.anad.org/get-information/about-eating-disorders/eating-disorders-statistics/.

"Eating Disorder Statistics." *South Carolina Department of Mental Health.* Accessed March 28, 2016. http://www.state.sc.us/dmh/anorexia/statistics.htm.

Ehrenfreund, Max. "17 Disturbing Statistics from the Federal Report on Ferguson Police." *WashingtonPost.com.* Posted March 4, 2015. Accessed February 2, 2016. http://www.washingtonpost.com/blogs/wonkblog/wp/2015/03/04/17-disturbing-statistics-from-the-federal-report-on-ferguson-police/.

"Facts About Suicide." *The Trevor Project* (website). Accessed April 5, 2016. http://www.thetrevorproject.org/pages/facts-about-suicide.

"Facts and Statistics About Infidelity." *Truth About Deception*. Accessed March 28, 2016. http://www.truthaboutdeception.com/cheating-and-infidelity/stats-about-infidelity.html.

Flegal, Katherine M., Brian K. Kit, Heather Orpana, and Barry I. Graubard. "Association of All-Cause Mortality with Overweight and Obesity Using Standard Body Mass Index Categories: A Systemic Review and Meta-analysis." *The Journal of the American Medical Association*, 309, no. 1 (2013): 71-82.

"Freud's Seduction Theory." *Wikipedia*. Accessed March 21, 2016. https://en.wikipedia.org/wiki/Freud%27s_seduction_theory.

Fryar, Cheryl D., Margaret D. Carroll, and Cynthia L. Ogden. "Prevalence of Obesity Among Children and Adolescents: United States, Trends 1963-1965 Through 2009-2010." *Centers for Disease Control and Prevention*. Posted November 6, 2015. Accessed March 21, 2016. http://www.cdc.gov/nchs/data/hestat/obesity_child_09_10/obesity_child_09_10.htm.

"Full Text of King's 'I Have a Dream' Speech." *ChicagoTribune.com*. Posted January 31, 2013. Accessed March 17, 2015. http://www.chicagotribune.com/news/nationworld/sns-mlk-ihaveadream-story.html#page=1.

Gaesser, Glenn A. *Big Fat Lies: The Truth About Your Weight and Your Health*. Carlsbad, CA: Gürze Books, 2002 [1996].

Garand, Linda, Jennifer H. Lingler, Kyaien O. Conner, and Mary Amanda Dew. "Diagnostic Labels, Stigma, and Participation in Research Related to Dementia and Mild Cognitive Impairment." *Research in Gerontological Nursing*, 2, no. 2 (2009): 112-121.

Garriga, Joshua. "Cornel West, Harvard, and the Pursuit of Greatness." *The Daily Garriga* (blog). Posted November 12, 2011. Accessed March 23, 2016. http://thedailygarriga.com/2011/11/12/cornel-west-harvard-and-the-pursuit-of-greatness/.

Gartrell, Nanette K., Henny M. W. Bos, and Naomi G. Goldberg. "Adolescents of the U.S. National Longitudinal Lesbian Family Study:

Sexual Orientation, Sexual Behavior, and Sexual Risk Exposure." *National Longitudinal Lesbian Family Study*. Posted June 4, 2010. Accessed March 28, 2016. https://www.nllfs.org/images/uploads/pdf/NLLFS-adolescents-sexuality-2010.pdf.

Gibson, David. "Five Myths About the Catholic Sexual Abuse Scandal." *WashingtonPost.com*. Posted April 18, 2010. Accessed March 28, 2016. http://www.washingtonpost.com/wp-dyn/content/article/2010/04/16/AR2010041602026.html.

Glassgold, Judith M., Lee Beckstead, Jack Drescher, Beverly Greene, Robin Lin Miller, and Roger L. Worthington. "Report of the American Psychological Association Task Force on Appropriate Therapeutic Response to Sexual Orientation." *American Psychological Association*. August 2009. Accessed March 28, 2016. http://www.apa.org/pi/lgbt/resources/therapeutic-response.pdf, 11.

Goffman, Erving. *Stigma: Notes on the Management of Spoiled Identity*. Englewood Cliffs, NJ: Prentice Hall, 1963.

Goldenberg, Suzanne. "Why Women Are Poor at Science, by Harvard President." *The Guardian*. Posted January 18, 2005. Accessed March 22, 2016. http://www.theguardian.com/science/2005/jan/18/educationsgendergap.genderissues.

Gray, John. *Men Are from Mars, Women Are from Venus: A Practical Guide for Improving Communication and Getting What You Want in Your Relationships*. New York: HarperCollins, 1992.

Grier, William H. and Price M. Cobbs. *Black Rage*. Eugene, OR: Wipf & Stock Publishers, 2000.

Griese, Noel L. "The Bible vs. Mao: A "Best Guess" of the Top 25 Bestselling Books of All Time." *Publishing Perspectives*. Posted September 7, 2010. Accessed March 8, 2016. http://publishingperspectives.com/2010/09/top-25-bestselling-books-of-all-time/.

Hagar, D. "People Pleaser." *Urban Dictionary*. Posted May 22, 2013. Accessed March 28, 2016. http://www.urbandictionary.com/define.php?term=people+pleaser.

Herek, Gregory M. "Facts About Homosexuality and Mental Health."

Sexual Orientation: Science, Education, and Policy. Accessed March 21, 2016. http://psc.dss.ucdavis.edu/rainbow/HTML/facts_mental_health.html.

Hughes, Langston. "Justice." *Poem Hunter.* Accessed March 28, 2016. http://www.poemhunter.com/poem/justice/.

Hunt, Jerome and Aisha C. Moodie-Mills. "The Unfair Criminalization of Gay and Transgender Youth." *Center for American Progress.* Posted June 29, 2012. Accessed March 28, 2016. https://www.americanprogress.org/issues/lgbt/report/2012/06/29/11730/the-unfair-criminalization-of-gay-and-transgender-youth/.

"Idiom: Death of a Thousand Cuts." *UsingEnglish.com.* Accessed April 5, 2016. http://www.usingenglish.com/reference/idioms/death+of+a+thousand+cuts.html.

"Interview with Beverly Daniel Tatum." *PBS.com.* Posted 2003. Accessed August 15, 2015. http://www.pbs.org/race/000_About/002_04-background-03-04.htm.

James, Susan Donaldson. "Honeymoon with Viagra Could Be over, Say Doctors." *ABCNews.com.* Posted June 9, 2011. Accessed March 28, 2016. http://abcnews.go.com/Health/viagra-prescription-sales-sexual-expectations/story?id=13794726.

Johnson, R. J. "Barack O'Hitler—The Right Wing's Favorite Past Time Debunked." *The Political Garbage Chute.* Posted January 28, 2013. Accessed March 28, 2016. http://www.politicalgarbagechute.com/barack-ohitler-the-right-wings-favorite-past-time-debunked/.

Jordan, June. *Technical Difficulties.* North Pomfret, VT: Trafalgar Square Books, 1993.

Jung, Carl G. "The Philosophical Tree." *Collected Works 13: Alchemical Studies.* 1945.

———. *The Red Book (Philemon).* Edited by Sonu Shamdasani. New York: W. W. Norton & Company, 2009.

Kann, Laura, Emily O'Malley Olsen, Tim McManus, Steve Kinchen, David Chyen, William A. Harris, and Howell Wechsler. "Sexual Identity, Sex of Sexual Contacts, and Health-Risk Behaviors Among Students in Grades 9-12: Youth Risk Behavior Surveillance, Selected Sites, United States, 2001-2009." *Division of Adolescent and School Health, National Center for Chronic Disease Prevention and Health Promotion, CDC.* Posted June 10, 2011. Accessed March 28, 2016. http://www.cdc.gov/mmwr/preview/mmwrhtml/ss6007a1.htm.

Kant, Garth. "Radical Increase in Kids Prescribed Ritalin." *WND.* Posted April 1, 2013. Accessed March 21, 2016. http://www.wnd.com/2013/04/radical-increase-in-kids-prescribed-ritalin/.

Katy. "The Problem with the Belief that Child Sexual Abuse *Causes* Homosexuality / Bisexuality." *Pandora's Project.* Posted 2009. Accessed March 28, 2016. http://www.pandys.org/articles/abuseandhomosexuality.html.

Kennard, Jerry. "The Pros and Cons of a Psychiatric Diagnosis." *Health Central.* Posted October 13, 2013. Accessed March 28, 2016. http://www.healthcentral.com/depression/c/4182/163428/cons-psychiatric-diagnosis/.

King, Jr., Martin Luther. "A Christmas Sermon on Peace, 1967." Accessed January 14, 2013. http://www.ecoflourish.com/Primers/education/Christmas_Sermon.html.

———. *Strength to Love.* Philadelphia: Fortress Press, 1963.

King, Lisa. "The Doping of America, Part 2: The Ritalin Generation." *Appalachian Chronicles.* Posted June 24, 2012. Accessed March 28, 2016. http://www.childrensbehaviorproblems.com/doping-american-kid-medicated-world/.

Kochan, Thomas A. "Microsoft CEO's Advice On Pay Raises Is Wrong For All (Not Just Women)." *Fortune.com.* Posted October 27, 2014. Accessed March 23, 2016. http://fortune.com/2014/10/27/microsoft-ceos-advice-on-pay-raises-is-wrong-for-all-not-just-women/.

Krans, Brian. "8 Ways Stress Is More Dangerous Than You Think." *Healthline News.* Posted August 27, 2013. Accessed March 15, 2015. http://www.healthline.com/health-news/mental-eight-ways-stress-harms-your-health-082713.

Larosa, John. "U.S. Weight Loss Market Worth $60.9 Billion." *PRWeb.*

Posted May 9, 2011. Accessed March 8, 2016. http://www.prweb.com/releases/2011/5/prweb8393658.htm.

Levine, Terry. "Sincere Ignorance and Conscientious Stupidity." *Terry Levine* (blog). Posted July 11, 2011. Accessed March 28, 2016. http://www.terrylevine.com/2011/07/sincere-ignorance-and-conscientious-stupidity.html.

Lichtblau, Eric. "The Holocaust Just Got More Shocking." *NYTimes.* Posted March 1, 2013. Accessed March 28, 2016. http://www.nytimes.com/2013/03/03/sunday-review/the-holocaust-just-got-more-shocking.html.

Link, Bruce G. and Jo C. Phelan. "Conceptualizing Stigma." *Annual Review of Sociology*, 27 (2001): 363–385.

Lo, Bernard and Marilyn J. Field, eds., *Conflict of Interest in Medical Research, Education, and Practice.* Washington, DC: Institute of Medicine of the National Academies Press, 2009. Accessed March 28, 2016. http://www.ncbi.nlm.nih.gov/books/NBK22942/pdf/Bookshelf_NBK22942.pdf.

Luchies, Laura B., Eli J. Finkel, James K. McNulty, Madoka Kumashiro. "The Doormat Effect: When Forgiving Erodes Self-Respect and Self-Concept Clarity." *Journal of Personality and Social Psychology*, 98 (2010): 734–749.

Lupton, Mary Jane. *Maya Angelou: A Critical Companion.* Westport, CT: Greenwood: 1998.

Mann, Traci, A. Janet Tomiyama, Erika Westling, Ann-Marie Lew, Barbra Samuels, and Jason Chatman. "Medicare's Search for Effective Obesity Treatments: Diets Are Not the Answer." *American Psychologist*, 62, no. 3 (2007): 220–233.

"Martin Luther King, Jr." *America's Story from America's Library.* Accessed March 17, 2015. http://www.americaslibrary.gov/aa/king/aa_king_subj.html.

"Maya Angelou Biography." *Academy of Achievement.* Posted May 28, 2014. Accessed March 28, 2016. http://www.achievement.org/autodoc/page/angobio-1.

McCristal Culp, Jr., Jerome. "Colorblind Remedies and the Intersectionality of Oppression: Policy Arguments Masquerading as Moral Claims." *New York University Law Review,* 69 no. 163 (1994): 164-165.

McNulty, James K. "The Dark Side of Forgiveness: The Tendency to Forgive Predicts Continued Psychological and Physical Aggression in Marriage." *Personality and Social Psychology Bulletin,* 37 (June 2011): 770-783.

McNutt, S. W., Y. Hu, G. B. Schreiber, P. B. Crawford, E. Obarzanek, and L. Mellin. "A Longitudinal Study of the Dietary Practices of Black and White Girls 9 and 10 Years Old at Enrollment: The NHLBI Growth and Health Study." *Journal of Adolescent Health,* 20, no. 1 (1997): 27-37.

Menken, Dawn. *Raising Parents, Raising Kids: Hands-on Wisdom for the Next Generation.* Santa Fe, NM: Belly Song Press, 2013.

Mindell, Amy. "Amy on the Evolution of Process Theory." *Amy and Arnold Mindell* (website). Posted Fall 2002. Accessed March 21, 2016. http://www.aamindell.net/1710/worldwork-terms/double-signals/.

Mindell, Arnold. *City Shadows: Psychological Interventions in Psychiatry.* Portland, OR: Lao Tse Press, 2009.

"Mindfulness: Present Moment Awareness." *PsychologyToday.com.* Accessed March 21, 2016. http://www.psychologytoday.com/basics/mindfulness.

Minuchin, Salvador. *Families and Family Therapy.* Cambridge, MA: Harvard University Press, 1974.

Moser, Fanny. *Spuk: Irrglaube oder Wahrglaube?* Foreword by C. G. Jung. Zurich: Gyr-Verlag, 1950.

Neal, Rome. "Caffeine Nation." *CBSNews.com.* Posted November 14, 2002. Accessed March 15, 2015. http://www.cbsnews.com/news/caffeine-nation/.

Neporent, Liz. "Childhood Obesity: Is 7 Too Young to Diet?" *ABCNews.com.* Posted March 12, 2013. Accessed February 15, 2016. http://abcnews.go.com/Health/childhood-obesity-young-diet/story?id=18704647&page=2.

Neruda, Pablo. "Keeping Quiet." *Extravagaria.* Translated by Alastair Reid. New York: Farrar, Straus and Giroux, 1974.

"Obesity and Mortality." *Obesity: Facts, Figures, Guidelines.* Accessed March 28, 2016. http://www.wvdhhr.org/bph/oehp/obesity/mortality.htm.

"Overweight and Obesity Statistics." *National Institute of Diabetes and Digestive and Kidney Diseases.* Posted October 2012. Accessed February 15, 2016. http://win.niddk.nih.gov/statistics/index.htm.

"Overweight Brides." *Dr. Phil.* CBS. January 12, 2005.

Phillips, Judson. "The State of the Union: Liberals Are the New Nazis." *Tea Party Nation.* Posted February 12, 2013. Accessed March 28, 2016. http://www.teapartynation.com/forum/topics/the-state-of-the-union-liberals-are-the-new-nazis.

Reiss, Gary. *Beyond War and Peace in the Arab Israeli Conflict.* Eugene, OR: Changing Worlds Publications, 2004.

Rice, Frances. "Why Dr. Martin Luther King, Jr. Was a Republican." *National Black Republican Association Newsletter.* Accessed January 13, 2013. http://suwanneegop.com/NBRA%20Civil%20Rights%20Newsletter-2.pdf.

Rilke, Rainer Maria. *The Book of Hours.* Translated by Robert Bly. Posted by *Nebraska Zen Center Heartland Temple.* Accessed March 28, 2016. http://www.prairiewindzen.org/zen_european_poetry.html.

Ritchie, Josh. "20 Tax Facts that Will Astonish You." *TurboTax Blog.* Posted July 13, 2011. Accessed March 28, 2016. http://blog.turbotax.intuit.com/tax-news/20-tax-facts-that-will-astonish-you-6665/.

Roan, Shari. "Keeping It Off." *LATimes.com.* Posted June 2, 2008. Accessed March 21, 2016. http://articles.latimes.com/2008/jun/02/health/he-regain2.

Ross, Carolyn Coker. "Why Do Women Hate Their Bodies?" *PsychCentral.com.* Posted June 1, 2012. Accessed January 16, 2013. http://psychcentral.com/blog/archives/2012/06/02/why-do-women-hate-their-bodies/.

"Satchel." *Black Lives Matter* video. Accessed August 15, 2015. http://blacklivesmatter.com/i-imagine-visions/satchel/. Page since deleted.

Schupbach, Max and Ellen. "Our Logo." *Deep Democracy Institute.*

Accessed March 21, 2016. http://www.deepdemocracyinstitute.org/
en/our-credo-our-logo/eventmont/2016/10.html.

Schwarz, Alan and Sarah Cohen. "A.D.H.D. Seen in 11% of U.S. Children
as Diagnoses Rise." *NYTimes.com*. Posted March 31, 2013. Accessed
March 21, 2016. http://www.nytimes.com/2013/04/01/health/more-
diagnoses-of-hyperactivity-causing-concern.html?pagewanted=all.

Selye, Hans. "Stress, in Addition to Being Itself, Was Also the Cause of
Itself, and the Result of Itself." *The American Institute of Stress*.
Accessed March 15, 2015. http://www.stress.org/management-tips/
#sthash.i9jqbZUu.dpuf.

Shange, Ntozake. *For Colored Girls Who Have Considered Suicide When the
Rainbow Is Enuf*. New York: Scribner, 1997.

"Shooting of Walter Scott." *Wikipedia*. Accessed February 2, 2016. https://
en.wikipedia.org/wiki/Shooting_of_Walter_Scott.

Silver, Mandy. "Cornel West Delivers 'Inspiring' Lecture." *Student Life*. Posted
February 3, 2006. Accessed March 21, 2016. http://www.studlife.com/
archives/News/2006/02/03/CornelWestdeliversinspiringlecture/.

Skolnick, Arlene. *The Intimate Environment: Exploring Marriage and the
Family*, 5th ed. New York: HarperCollins, 1992.

"Sleep Tips: 7 Steps to Better Sleep." *Mayo Clinic*. Posted June 9, 2014.
Accessed March 15, 2015. http://www.mayoclinic.org/healthy-living/
adult-health/in-depth/sleep/art-20048379?pg=1.

"The Slow and Tortured Death of Affirmative Action." *The Black Commentator* (blog). Accessed March 28, 2016. http://www.blackcommentator.
com/49/49_cover.html.

Spake, Amanda. "Stop Dieting! Forget the Scale, the Calorie Counting,
and Forbidden Foods. They May Be Doing More Harm Than Good."
USNews.com. Posted January 8, 2006. Accessed October 31, 2011.
http://health.usnews.com/usnews/health/articles/060116/16diet.
htm (page since deleted).

"Stop-and-Frisk Data." *New York Civil Liberties Union*. Accessed March 28,
2016. http://www.nyclu.org/content/stop-and-frisk-data.

"Stress Management Health Center: Reducing Stress, Stress Symptoms,

Causes, Treatments, and Relief." *WebMD*. Posted March 15, 2015. http://www.webmd.com/balance/stress-management/.

"Stress Symptoms: Effects on Your Body and Behavior." *Mayo Clinic*. Posted July 19, 2013. Accessed May 15, 2015. http://www.mayoclinic.org/healthy-living/stress-management/in-depth/stress-symptoms/art-20050987.

Swanson, Ana. "Whites Greatly Overestimate the Share of Crimes Committed by Black People." *WashingtonPost.com*. Posted December 1, 2014. Accessed February 2, 2016. http://www.washingtonpost.com/blogs/wonkblog/wp/2014/12/01/whites-greatly-overestimate-the-share-of-crimes-committed-by-black-people/.

Tatum, Beverly Daniel. *Why Are All the Black Kids Sitting Together in the Cafeteria? And Other Conversations About Race.* New York: Basic Books, 2003.

Taylor, Jared. *Paved With Good Intentions: The Failure of Race Relations in Contemporary America.* New York: Carroll & Graf Publishers, 1993.

Throckmorton, Warren. "Mark Driscoll's Real Marriage and Robert Brannon's Male Sex Roles: Coincidence or Something More?" *Patheos*. Posted January 23, 2014. Accessed March 21, 2016. http://www.patheos.com/blogs/warrenthrockmorton/2014/01/23/mark-driscolls-real-marriage-and-robert-brannons-male-sex-roles-coincidence-or-something-more/.

Turner, Erick H., Annette M. Matthews, Eftihia Linardatos, Robert A. Tell, and Robert Rosenthal. "Selective Publication of Antidepressant Trials and Its Influence on Apparent Efficacy." *The New England Journal of Medicine*, 358, no. 3 (2008). Accessed March 28, 2016. http://www.nejm.org/doi/full/10.1056/NEJMsa065779.

Turner, Ronald. "Misusing MLK Legacy and the Colorblind Theory – II. Martin Luther King, Jr.'s Color-Awareness." *Race, Racism and the Law*. Accessed March 28, 2016. http://www.racism.org/index.php?option=com_content&view=article&id=869:justice06-1&catid=143&Itemid=120&showall=&limitstart=2.

University of Nebraska-Lincoln. "How Our Brains See Men as People and

Women as Body Parts: Both Genders Process Images of Men, Women Differently." *Science Daily*. Posted July 25, 2012. Accessed March 23, 2016. www.sciencedaily.com/releases/2012/07/120725150215.htm.

Uwujaren, Jarune. "If You 'Don't See Race,' You're Not Paying Attention." *Everyday Feminism*. Posted September 11, 2013. Accessed August 15, 2015. http://everydayfeminism.com/2013/09/dont-see-race/.

Ventura, Michael. "Letters at 3am: James Hillman (1926-2011): Remembering James Hillman." *AustinChronicle.com*. Posted January 13, 2012. Accessed March 21, 2016. http://www.austinchronicle.com/columns/2012-01-13/letters-at-3am-james-hillman-1926-2011/.

Walters, Karina L. and Jane M. Simoni. "Reconceptualizing Native Women's Health: An "Indigenist" Stress-Coping Model." *American Journal of Public Health*, 92, no. 4 (2002): 520-524.

Washington, James Melvin. ed. "A Slave Woman's Prayer (1816)." Found by Stephen Hays. *Conversations with God: Two Centuries of Prayers by African Americans*. New York: HarperPerennial, 1994.

Wattrick, Jeff. "Yes, Henry Payne, Martin Luther King Really Did Support Affirmative Action." *Deadline Detroit*. Posted August 28, 2013. Accessed March 28, 2016. http://www.deadlinedetroit.com/articles/ 6195/ yes_henry_payne_martin_luther_king_really_did_support_affirmative_action#.VLV_cUvOXKA.

Weekend Edition Sunday. "At 80, Maya Angelou Reflects on a 'Glorious' Life." *NPR.org*. Posted April 6, 2008. Accessed April 5, 2016. http://www.npr.org/2008/04/06/89355359/at-80-maya-angelou-reflects-on-a-glorious-life.

Weeks, James. "Crazy or Not Crazy?" *Across the King's River*. Posted June 17, 2014. Accessed March 28, 2016. http://www.acrossthekingsriver.com/crazy-or-not-crazy/.

West, Cornel. *Hope on a Tightrope*. New York: Smiley Books, 2008.

———. *Never Forget: A Journey of Revelations*. Los Angeles: Hidden Beach Records, 2007, compact disc.

———. *Restoring Hope: Conversations on the Future of Black America*. Boston: Beacon Press, 1997.

Whittington, Craig J., Tim Kendall, Peter Fonagy, David Cottrell, Andrew Cotgrove, and Ellen Boddington. "Selective Serotonin Reuptake Inhibitors in Childhood Depression: Systematic Review of Published Versus Unpublished Data." *The Lancet,* 363, no. 9418 (2004): 1341–1345. Accessed March 28, 2016. http://www.thelancet.com/pdfs/journals/lancet/PIIS0140673604160431.pdf.

Willis, Oliver. "ADL Criticizes "Inappropriate" Holocaust References from Conservative Media During Gun Debate." *Media Matters for America.* Posted January 24, 2013. Accessed March 28, 2016. http://mediamatters.org/blog/2013/01/24/adl-criticizes-inappropriate-holocaust-referenc/192383.

Winerman, Lea. "Helping Men to Help Themselves." *American Psychological Association.* Posted June 2005. Accessed March 22, 2016. http://www.apa.org/monitor/jun05/helping.aspx.

Winnicott, D. W. "Ego Distortion in Terms of True and False Self." *The Maturational Process and the Facilitating Environment: Studies in the Theory of Emotional Development.* New York: International UP Inc., 1965: 140–152.

Wiviott, Gerald. "The Psychology of Fundamentalism." Accessed March 23, 2016. http://infosect.freeshell.org/infocult/The_Psychology_of_Fundamentalism-Gerald_Wiviott.pdf.

Zhong, Chen-Bo. "The Ethical Dangers of Rational Decision Making." *Academy of Management Proceedings.* Posted August 1, 2008. Accessed March 23, 2016. https://www.gsb.stanford.edu/sites/default/files/documents/Zhong_Ethical_Dangers.pdf

Index

About the Author

David Bedrick, J.D., Dipl. PW, is a speaker, teacher, and attorney and author of the acclaimed *Talking Back to Dr. Phil: Alternatives to Mainstream Psychology*. He spent eight years on the faculty of the University of Phoenix and has taught for the U.S. Navy, 3M, psychological associations, and small groups. He has received notable awards for teaching, employee development, and legal service to the community.

David completed graduate work in psychology at the University of Minnesota and clinical training at the Process Work Institute, where he is a diplomate and adjunct faculty member as well as a member of the ethics committee and the advisory board for the master of arts program in conflict facilitation. As a practitioner of process-oriented psychology, a branch of Jungian psychology, he has worked with groups, couples, and individuals for over twenty years.

David currently maintains an international private practice as a counselor for individuals, couples, and groups and works via Skype, phone, or in person in Santa Fe, New Mexico. He speaks and teaches on topics ranging from shame, night time dreams, weight loss and body image, diversity and social injustice, and alternatives to popular psychology and is a blogger for *Psychology Today* and *The Huffington Post*.